Art Center College of Design
Library
1700 Lida Street
Pasadena, Calif. 91103

D0743122

ART CENTER COLLEGE OF DESIGN

3 3220 00237 4879

REF.
629.2275Ø973
Z 71
2003

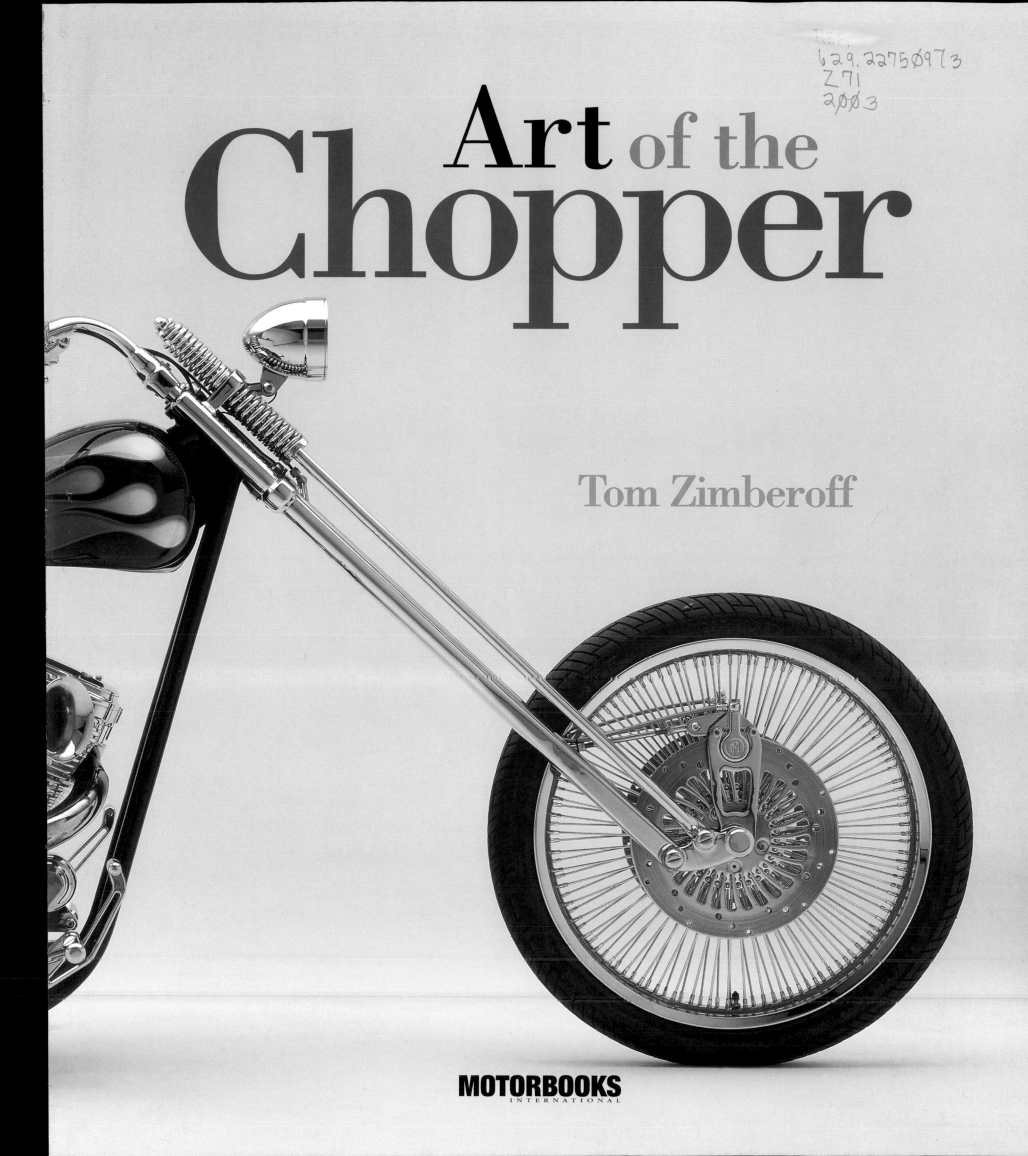

Art of the
Chopper

Tom Zimberoff

MOTORBOOKS
INTERNATIONAL

This edition first published in 2003 by Motorbooks International, an imprint of MBI Publishing Company, Galtier Plaza, Suite 200, 380 Jackson Street, St. Paul, MN 55101-3885 USA

© Tom Zimberoff, 2003

All rights reserved. With the exception of quoting brief passages for the purposes of review, no part of this publication may be reproduced without prior written permission from the Publisher.

The information in this book is true and complete to the best of our knowledge. All recommendations are made without any guarantee on the part of the author or Publisher, who also disclaim any liability incurred in connection with the use of this data or specific details.

We recognize that some words, model names and designations, for example, mentioned herein are the property of the trademark holder. We use them for identification purposes only. This is not an official publication.

Motorbooks International titles are also available at discounts in bulk quantity for industrial or sales-promotional use. For details write to Special Sales Manager at Motorbooks International Wholesalers & Distributors, Galtier Plaza, Suite 200, 380 Jackson Street, St. Paul, MN 55101-3885 USA.

ISBN 0-7603-1572-8

Edited by Darwin Holmstrom
Cover deisgned by Tom Heffron
Interior designed by Becky Pagel and Mandy Iverson

Printed in Hong Kong

Photo Notes

Equipment:

Three venerable Leica M4 cameras were used to create all of the b+w candids. I used four Leitz lenses: 21mm, 35mm, 135mm, and 50mm.

For the 35mm color, which required less stalking, longer lenses, and a greater capability to capture action I relied on my motorized Canon EOS 1 with a 20-35mm zoom and a 80-200mm zoom.

The black-and-white portraits and color bike illustrations alike were made with a 4x5 Wista SP Technical Camera and three lenses: a 135 Nikkor, a 150mm Schneider, and a 210 Nikkor. The Copal/Wista shutter with interlinking mechanism to the film back on the camera made focusing more feasible by automatically stopping down the aperture to a predetermined value.

Even in an increasingly digital world, no image can exist without the film to make it possible, if you want the extraordinary quality yielded by a large-format camera and the certainty that you can view your images fifty-plus years from now. For that kind of confidence I relied on Kodak T-Max 100 for the portraits, Tri-X 400 35mm for the candids, and E100-S, both 35mm and 4x5 for every color photograph with a motorcycle in it. All 4x5 film used was in Readyload packets.

Four Speedotron 4800 flash units and as many heads provided artificial light.

A Chimera F2 collapsible light bank, five feet wide by ten feet long, provided illumination for the bike illustrations, with help from Matthews C-stands, High-rollers, booms, sandbags, flags, gobos, and other grip equipment in various combinations.

ART CENTER COLLEGE OF DESIGN LIBRARY

Contents

Chrome Magnum
Alan Lee

Untitled
Eddie Trotta

Foreword

By Ralph "Sonny" Barger

WHEN WE STARTED CUSTOMIZING HARLEY BIG TWINS IN THE LATE 1950S, most of the dealers banned us from their shops and wouldn't sell parts to us. We were trying to make the bikes run faster by shedding excess weight off them and give them a cooler, more streamlined look. But they thought what we were doing was an outrage, destroying the stock bikes.

So it tickles me that four decades later well-off people are spending big bucks for choppers, and they are considered "art" worthy of display in museums. They started out as poor boys' toys.

Some of the one-percenter clubs have even had rules from time to time that their members must ride choppers and not what we called "garbage wagons." This was in stark contrast to the touring clubs and riders shown in Harley ads back then.

We would first take the front fenders entirely off, cut the back fender down, and change the handle bars. The earliest pullback bars were the bent chromed steel tubes from a style of kitchen chair legs popular in that era. One of the first aftermarket accessory companies, Flanders, made risers and handle bars you could put on a rigid front end. But mostly we had to make parts from scratch or adapt what we had, like cutting off a rigid front end and welding it to another, making it six inches longer. There was a tire cover off a 1936 Ford truck that made a beautiful back fender for a sixteen-inch tire on a Harley. Or you could cut the front fender of a Hydra-Glide and mount it backwards to create a sharp-looking rear fender.

The photo on page 9 shows me in 1960 on a bike I built that year, an eighty-inch stroker. The dual carbs were welded directly onto the heads so I didn't have to make a manifold. Using fork tubes from a Hydra-Glide that were turned down on a lathe and triple clamps that were narrowed a couple of inches made the front end look a lot like the current narrow glides. Everything that could be chromed was chromed, and the yellow flamed paint job was by Red Lee. It was a radical bike for that time, ran very fast, and I traded it in the next year for a brand new Sportster which didn't remain stock for very long at all.

It was about that time one of our members in Oakland got in a wreck, and I stripped his bike and made a chopper out of it for him while he was in the hospital.

We cut the flywheels down to make them lighter and allow quicker acceleration. Heavier flywheels may be better at the top end, but everyone wanted to accelerate. For more speed, we punched out the carburetors and put in cams, solid push rods, bigger valves, different gears in the transmission, and bigger sprockets.

The wide gas tanks and cushy upholstered seats of the stock bikes covered up the motor. We liked showing the motor off (and being able to get at it), so we switched to much smaller tanks and little seats placed directly on the frame and part of the rear fender. It was much more important to look cool than to have a long cruising range or to be comfortable.

Extending the front ends got to be something of a competition in itself, to see how far you could go. My personal preference is for good handling on the road and street, and I have never run more than a 3½-inch extension with no rake.

Admittedly some of the more extreme customization has safety implications, so the rider who understands and accepts these risks must have kind of a daredevil attitude. That must be another reason why we do it.

Now it is possible, for folks with enough money, to build custom bikes from a wide choice of components readily available on the market. There are even some alternatives to Milwaukee motors, and all kinds of new parts are possible only because of modern materials and high-tech manufacturing.

Some of the bikes in this book are well suited for the racetrack, others for cruising, and some just for looking at. Each of them is a unique expression of its builder's vision of styling and performance. Whether you call them transportation or art, they are all about one thing: *fun*.

—July 2003 Ralph "Sonny" Barger
Phoenix, Aizona

Ralph "Sonny" Barger, a founding member of the Oakland Hell's Angels in 1957, has been a leading figure in the motorcycle community for more than four decades and is the author of several books, including *Hell's Angel: The Life and Times of Sonny Barger and the Hell's Angels Motorcycle Club*, which is being developed as a major motion picture by Twentieth Century Fox to be directed by Tony Scott.

ART CENTER COLLEGE OF DESIGN LIBRARY

Introduction

THE WORLD OF HIGH FASHION IS DOMINATED BY A SMALL NUMBER OF *COUTURIERS* whose glamorous, one-of-a-kind, over-the-top, and extravagantly expensive apparel debuts each season with much fanfare in the salons of cosmopolitan capitals throughout the world. From runway to rack, their designs initiate a process of trickle-down style in which Wal-mart copies dominate sales. The motorcycle industry, too, pays close attention to the seasonal splash of high-priced, high fashion at similarly aggrandized media events. Only instead of the runways of Paris, Milan, Tokyo, and New York, I give you the streets of Sturgis, Daytona, Hollister, and Milwaukee. Instead of anorexic models wearing the latest Givency, Dior, Miyake, Armani, and Versace, I give you the steroid- and silicone-enhanced bodies epitomized by professional wrestlers and strippers astride the trendsetting creations of the builders represented within these pages. But this book is not about people who ride motorcycles *per se*, or the hedonistic lives they might lead. It's about guys who *build* $70,000 motorcycles to die for. It's about their legerdemain with sheet metal, and their legendary personas. It's not about biker culture—it's about how these bikes *are* culture.

Zimberoff and Billy Lane. **Tony Irvin**

Opposite Zimberoff and Chica. **Tony Irvin**

11

Zimberoff and Arlen Ness. Tony Irvin

Psychedelic Shovel
Tom Rad

Choppers are literally vehicles of self expression. Their creators have a talent for carving, pounding, and welding solid blocks of aluminum and sheet metal into art that moves, and moves the beholder. Handcrafting motorcycles is as much a way of life as a business. In his book *Zen and the Art of Motorcycle Maintenance*, Robert Persig wrote, "The ancient Greeks never separated art from manufacture in their minds, and so never developed separate words for them. Actually a root word of technology, *techne*, originally *meant* 'art.'" That fits the bill nicely.

Custom builders are the arbiters of change in the world of commercially produced motorcycles. What they define as high fashion—or, as the case may be, cool, trick, or bitchin'—will eventually drift down into the corporate abyss of mass production and media hyperbole. Nevertheless, this volume celebrates their work as more than mere popular entertainment. The building and riding of choppers is an American art form as indigenous as jazz. Its improvised riffs have given rise to as many mechanical doodads, chrome thingamajigs, bars, frames, forks, tanks, and tires—and different ways to combine them—as there are notes in a Charlie Parker saxophone solo. And with the exportation of these kinds of eccentricities to other cultures, chopper style has become as recognizable in Riyadh as in Rochester.

But if I may put that simile aside, I began this introduction with a testament to choppers as high fashion, and I'd like to stick with it. It's not the kind of fashion you'll see in *Vogue*. Instead of décolletage, you're going to get stretch in the top tube. Instead of chiffon and taffeta, you're going to get chrome and iron. Instead of the allure of *haute couture*, I give you a grittier glamour in the name of *haute moteur*: *Art of the Chopper*.

There's a line in Quentin Tarrantino's film *Pulp Fiction* in which Butch, a boxer played by Bruce Willis, corrects his girlfriend: "It's not a motorcycle; it's a chopper," he scolds. It is a remarkable comment in the context of a film that is as fashionably cool as is it notorious for the gruesomeness it ignores with a vengeance. It violently demands your attention for the sake of art. It is the motion picture equivalent of a chopper.

Psychedelic Shovel
Tom Rad

Choppers too demand attention. If you park the latest Ducati, Honda, Yamaha, BMW, or stock Harley-Davidson on a street corner in any city or town in the world, only a few passersby may pay much attention. But bring on a slammed-to-the-ground, stretched and raked-out, big-bore V-twin chopper bedizened with blinding chrome, pipes out the wahzoo, and a radical paint job and you will indeed attract a crowd! Such a motorcycle, like any other coveted work of art, becomes the center of attention wherever it rolls into public view. An object for contemplation, not mere transportation, choppers are paradoxical. They are the sacramental objects of a culture that worships profanity. They are vulgar and ostentatious, and yet achingly beautiful. Their presence will always provoke opinionated remarks, as will any object of desire. Incidentally, never would a rider park one where he couldn't keep an eye on it; not for fear that it might be purloined, but because every parking spot represents a new tableau to enjoy.

Today, baby-boomers have instigated a renaissance in the high art of the low rider, the chopper's unruly but stylish combination of iron, oil, chrome, paint, rubber, and decibels. But, whereas some people are satisfied with what comes off the rack, say, a stock Harley

Zimberoff at work. **Tony Irvin**

Zimberoff and the Martin Brothers. **Tony Irvin**

with a daub of chrome here and a smattering of extra horsepower there, or even a "Wal-Mart" chopper, a connoisseur will demand something tailor made, something jaw-droppingly different at a commensurably one-of-a-kind, jaw-dropping price. Owning and riding a custom chopper is an egomaniacal self-indulgence. As Eddie Trotta says, "It's better to look good than feel good!" But it also represents a defiant stance against mediocrity and conformity, as long as you have the pecuniary clout to turn substance into style just for the hell of it.

Owning a custom chopper is the dream of many riders. The word *custom* implies a high degree of individuality and a paragon of style; that is to say it has all the characteristics of being hand crafted after a unique design. It has panache. Picture the difference between a Ford and a Ferrari. Now, put the body of a top-fuel dragster on the Ferrari and add about a gazillion horsepower! By contrast, the Harley-Davidson Motor Company refers to "custom" what the actual riders of custom bikes call "billet barges."[1] Many are good looking to be sure. And they are distinctive; but only insofar as one bone-stock Harley looks pretty much like any other without the addition of bolt-on accessories. Therein lies the verisimilitude of so many motorcycles cluttered with chrome. They are not customized; they are *personalized*.

Now consider the term *chopper*. Just the opposite of billet barge, it was coined to describe the kinds of motorcycles from which superfluous parts have been removed, or chopped off, to give them the clean and uncluttered lines consistent with the aesthetic

Chrome Magnum
Alan Lee

Triumph
Tom Rad

and historical values their riders enjoy. They have an obvious Harley heritage (i.e., the V-twin motor, the rhythmic rumble of the exhaust, the chrome, and the arms-out, knees-to-the-breeze riding position), but they also have an edge that is more avant garde than the enduring expression of Harley's 1903 legacy.

Not to get into the history of choppers here, but at first they weren't so much *built* as they were deconstructed from stock motorcycles. Chopper style, to be technically correct, is the result of a subtractive process. A chopper "builder" strips machines designed and mass produced by corporate culture to their bare essentials, hops up the horsepower to make them faster, which of course is socially unacceptable, and adds a few innovations and embellishments to make each one unique. When all the trappings of factory decoration and government-mandated conformity come off (gewgaws, gauges, reflectors, and flashing lights), the result should reflect one person's subjective vision with a dissimilitude that is the mechanical equivalent of a wild animal staking out it's territory.

It once seemed to me that the be all and end all of motorcycling was to own a Harley-Davidson. The idea of owning and riding a Harley a dozen years ago seemed like a radical proposition to most people. The contributions of the Harley-Davidson Motor Company are still at the core of motivation for innovation within the industry. The *real* American Idle, if you will, is *potato-potato-potato*. But the enormous success of Harley-Davidson in recent years has led to hard-ass bikers rubbing shoulders with the mainstream of society and not liking it. Riding has almost become wholesome again.

Zimberoff and Chica. **Tony Irvin**

Regardless, immediately after I got my first Harley the word *stock* acquired a new significance in my vocabulary. This new and somewhat disparaging meaning struck blows to my bank account and my ego. Drinkers and gamblers, overeaters and sex addicts alike can find empathy within groups of repentant peers; but a Harley-Davidson owner is destined to skulk forever in the purgatory of one-upmanship. To buy a Harley-Davidson motorcycle is merely to put a down payment on the parts you'll have to buy to make yours look unique. The next step up from *personalizing* a Harley is to buy or build a custom motorcycle. When you're ready to reach for the top shelf, it's time to visit a custom chopper builder.

Savior
Mike Brown

Today, although the culture of cool is prevalent, the idea of literally chopping up an old bike to give it a new look seldom holds true, because chopper style today is less representative of what it once was and more so a vision of what it will be in the future. The so-called "old school" is matriculating to higher education. Existing stock bikes aren't so much modified as they are begun from scratch with a particular "chopped" look in mind. Still, all modern choppers are *derived* from old-school choppers based on the classic Harley-Davidson design. Exemplars of chopper style have always probed for increasingly radical ways to express the idea that less is more.

Indeed, each chopper is a kind of motorhead haiku, a biker's best expression of beauty. Although it is by no means as subtle,

YHVH
Mike Brown

the best examples are poetry in motion nonetheless. To wit, look at the innovative work Mike Brown is doing in Tennessee, bound to influence the look of choppers to come when it hits the streets. Contrast his bikes with those of Tom Rad in Minnesota, who builds them as if time had stood still. Somewhere between futuristic and quaint lies what I like to call the *art techno* work of Europeans such as Alan Lee from Belgium.

Choppers aren't *back*—they've been around for forty years. The only difference is that the media has discovered them. (That's almost a pun.) Their popularity with the general public and riders alike will wax and wane with hemlines and double-breasted suits. Chopper style continues to evolve in all kinds of directions.

According to Jason Martin, the recent influence of cable television on the popularity of choppers helped people understand that, "When they're buying a bike from a true builder, they're not buying a motorcycle. They're buying a representation of that artist." Martin believes that TV performed a service to the industry. It explained for the first time to a large audience, not just the rationale for owning a chopper, but it also justified how much time it takes and how much it costs to build one by hand.

There are any number of mechanics who can bolt a bike together. There are many talented fabricators and painters too. But those who can combine these disparate ingredients and subordinate them to a singular vision of motorcycle artistry are few and far between. They are here for you to see in this book.

ART CENTER COLLEGE OF DESIGN LIBRARY

[1] Billet is bulk aluminum that is sculpted by computer-controlled machines into accessories and performance parts of exacting proportions and polished to a high sheen. It is often mistaken for chrome.

Chapter 1

Mitch Bergeron

The Thrill of the Build

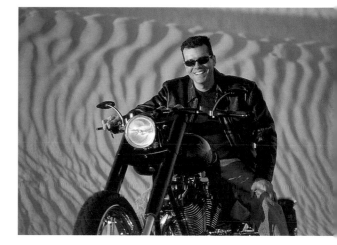

A MODEST MAN WHO VALUES THE ECONOMY OF HIS WORDS, Mitch Bergeron finds it hard to talk about his own bikes. He is obsessed with quality. The effort he invests in each motorcycle he lays hands on is evident in its details and the obvious and satisfying interrelationship between parts. He works to create a framework—literally the chassis of the motorcycle—that allows the various other component parts to work in harmony.

Bergeron prowls through public libraries and bookstores looking for examples of striking graphics—even in kid's books—to give him inspiration. "I've done so many bikes, I can visualize what it's going to look like in the end," he says. That includes his ability to visualize what *won't* look good, too, such as when clients come to him with wish lists. Mitch laughs when he thinks of how customers try to exert their influence over him. "I usually work out a game plan with them," he says. Like every other builder, he's happy when his customers are happy. But if he were to let some follow their own inexpert advice, they would likely wind up with a clumsy-looking motorcycle. Bergeron hates to hear gratuitous suggestions for the use of a part or a technique just because someone saw it on TV or in a magazine; so he'll try to cajole customers into letting him do things his way.

"Once I've finished a bike, I want it out of here," says Bergeron, who maintains little sentimentality for his creations. "It's only a mechanical thing. I get tired of it fast. I put a lot of time and effort into making it unique, but when it's done, it's done."

Like many builders, Bergeron's work leaves less time for riding than he'd like. "I like the thrill of the build. That's my thing." He appreciates bikers' "live to ride, ride to live" motto, their commitment to cowboy-like freedom. "It sounds corny as hell, but I think that's what the true biker is [a cowboy]."

When asked whose work he most admires, he says, "If I lost both my arms and couldn't build myself one, I'd go see Exile Cycles. I like their style; it's clean and simplified. Billy Lane would be one, too."

When asked if a great motorcycle could be built from a parts catalog, Bergeron replies, "Not really, I guess, because then anybody could do it. If a person has a good eye, he can build himself a real nice machine. Grant you, it won't be different."

Bergeron himself started building bikes professionally during the 1990s, when everybody had money to burn. After a couple of gigs at other bike shops, he opened his own place of business in Montreal, Quebec, in 1995. He specialized in creating custom rolling chassis and sheet metal. It was at this time that he began his collaboration with famed painter Martin Bouchard, known as "Fitto." The bikes the pair created won awards right and left.

The early bikes Bergeron built before starting his own shop were, he recalls, "Fantasy bikes almost with everything covered, everything hidden. It was a real pain in the ass if the bike ever had a mechanical problem, because you had to unbolt 20 panels to get to it." When he started building his own bikes, he gravitated towards the choppers then popular in Scandinavia.

Bergeron thinks that while Americans are over the moon right now about choppers, the Europeans are already thinking ahead stylistically. He thinks they might come back with a cleaned-up body bike and re-export the style to America: "Less body, but maybe same stance." Fat and low may come back, but with a look simplified by the chopper experience.

The frame of a motorcycle is the most important part to Bergeron. "I like doing one-offs," he says. "Be it a chopper frame or a low digger, I want the frame to be neutral, so you can build a bike *around* it." The frames he makes today are clean enough so that they don't overpower any bike stylistically.

Like most builders, Bergeron finds it easy to identify the work of other master builders; each usually has at least one signature styling touch. In particular, he recognizes their work by the shapes of their sheet metal and the finishing touches. Ironically, he cannot articulate that kind of clarity about his own work. "I don't see my own style," he says. He believes he is still defining his style. "I try to change all the time," he says. "It's a bad business move, but I really *really* hate doing the same thing over."

Bergeron obtained his motorcycle license practically within hours of his 16th birthday, the earliest age at which he could earn a license in Alberta, Canada, where he grew up. Shortly thereafter, he bought his first 100-cc basket case motorcycle. He had already begun reading *Easyriders*, too. "Mom didn't like that," he says, referring to the semi-nude beauties draped over the motorcycles featured in the magazine. Anyway, he made that little 100 run. He would crash it, and make it run again. Eventually he bought a bigger bike, and finally he acquired a Harley Sportster.

Mitch Bergeron recently moved from Montreal, Quebec, where he had started his business, to the United States. Doing business in Quebec became a tough proposition. The authorities seem to have torn the 1970s chapter out of an American history book and are trying to relive it. Throughout Quebec, according to Bergeron, nothing with over a 35-degree rake is allowed on the streets. "I couldn't pull one [of my bikes] out of the driveway, basically," says Mitch. Each custom bike is measured by the Quebecois authorities before it can be registered. Once, Mitch's bike failed to pass the criteria simply because it had chrome handgrips! If the bike to be registered doesn't match a photograph of a stock Harley-Davidson the bureaucrats keep for comparison, it fails. "If you do succeed in registering a custom bike, there's still an enormous insurance hurdle to jump. You just can't get insurance commensurate with the value of your motorcycle."

Mitch and his wife packed up the shop equipment on a couple of skids and drove to California where they set up shop near Palm Springs. Now that he's practicing his craft in the motorcycle Mecca of California, Mitch Bergeron has no problems registering his wild choppers.

Untitled

Untitled

ART CENTER COLLEGE OF DESIGN LIBRARY

Thor

Chapter 2

Roger Bourget

Longer, Lower, Leaner and Meaner

ROGER BOURGET HAS A VERY SPECIFIC IDEA OF WHAT CONSTITUTES A CHOPPER. "To me a chopper is a motorcycle that's stretched out over stock length. Neck height is at least four inches above what a stock bike would be. And [it should have] a rake of forty-two degrees or more."

"Everybody's looking for something different," Bouget says, "something to set himself apart. The old-school guys used to chop the chassis and kick the front end out just to draw attention to themselves. Basically, that's the whole idea."

Two visual factors distinguish Bourget's chopper designs. The first is that Bourget's frames contain all vital fluids. Because his patented frames are manufactured from wider-than-normal tubing, they can accommodate oil lubricating and cooling systems that pump fluid through the frame itself. This eliminates the need for a separate oil reservoir under the seat.

The oil-in-frame design gives Bourget's choppers their second distinguishing feature. The absence of an "oil bag" allows the seat on a Bourget bike to be lowered to an unprecedented extent and achieve a butt-scraping riding position.

Along with the drop seat and oil-in-the-frame design, Bourget was one of the first to introduce big rubber in the rear to give the traffic in back the impression of a man riding down the street on a big, fat tire. Back in 1991, he was building chopper frames that accommodated Corvette and Viper automobile tires.

The fundamental design for all of Bourget's motorcycles stems from a fortuitous circumstance: the stature of Roger's wife Brigitte. Roger wanted to teach her how to ride. At five feet, three inches tall, she had a hard time planting her feet on the ground astride a typical Harley. Wheels started turning in Roger's head when the new Harley-Davidson Dyna chassis debuted. This design allowed the oil pan to fit underneath the transmission and left room to chop the frame and lower the seat.

Bourget built his first two project bikes in his garage in the early 1980s. Both of them were big-tire choppers and were featured in magazines.

He soon discovered that he could design bikes as well build them. After the owner of the Harley shop where Roger worked introduced him to computer numeric control (CNC) machining, Roger locked himself in a room, read the manuals, and taught himself to program the computer software necessary to make wheels, forward controls, and triple trees. When he realized the potential of this technology, he knew he wanted to build motorcycles for a living. To make it lucrative enough he knew he had to design his own components, which he could do with CNC technology.

His first Harley, a 1984 Softail he bought in fall of 1983, changed him. "I started getting into the culture and the way bikes looked. I started looking at what Ness and Simms were doing and—actually Pat Kennedy was a pretty big influence on me."

Roger says he wanted to build the kind of motorcycle he could park at Sturgis and still be able to find. Riding the first chopper he built was nerve-wracking. He likens the experience to the flights of early aviators. They were confident in their work, but they didn't *know* if they could stay up in the air.

Although he's not a motor guy, Roger can put one together in a pinch, but his forte has always been design. Bourget's one-off bikes hover within the $60,000 to $80,000 price range. "A lot of guys still like to ride hard tails," says Bourget. "If everybody had the type of roads that we have out here [in Arizona] and in Florida, I think every guy would want to ride a hard tail. That's just my opinion. It's such a better looking bike, lower and cleaner."

Roger believes that people who ride motorcycles—choppers in particular—take risks, but not lightly. It's a matter of choice, experiencing life to the fullest, and not taunting death. And if you ride, you want to look damn good doing it! Roger rides for relaxation, but his schedule makes it hard to participate in organized group rides. His putts are usually impromptu.

Bourget has received a lot of attention from television, which he considers both a blessing and a challenge. The publicity is good for business, but catering to the cameras takes time away from personal and family pursuits. "I just don't appreciate when—for entertainment purposes—it [the media] makes a lot of us who are very professional look like misfits."

Despite the current popularity surrounding choppers today, Bourget isn't certain about what trends are in store for choppers and is somewhat pessimistic about their survivability, not as a form of artistic expression, but as a going concern within the marketplace. He's not sure if businesses can support the current demand for and popularity of choppers because it is becoming harder to insure bikes like these. That makes it difficult for manufacturers and their dealers to sell them. It's becoming more difficult to meet Department of Transportation regulations, as well. Bourget worries about how long the government will let him keep building motorcycles his way.

When asked if he'd buy a bike from another builder, Bourget says, "I think I'd probably buy a bike from Pat [Kennedy], honestly. I hate to say this. I've never really told this to anybody, but I liked his style; his *Alien* bike and the stuff he did back then. It still would be cool now. I like the fact that he doesn't build any two the same. At my position now in life, if I wanted to buy something, I'd want something pretty one-off."

Roger Bourget's personal looks are as distinctive as his choppers. After a ride back from Laughlin some years ago, his shoulder-length locks got terribly tangled and knotted. After Brigitte tried to comb them out unsuccessfully, the only option was to cut them off. He kept cutting and cutting, and then got out a razor. He kept his scalp scraped for quite a while, but Roger didn't like his head totally shaved because he didn't like wearing a hat in the summer to protect himself from sunburn. So he thought he'd leave a little bit of hair on top to keep the sun off. People said it suited him, and he agreed. That was it: a new look. Now the Mohawk mane he wears is as much a Bourget trademark as his distinctive choppers.

Untitled

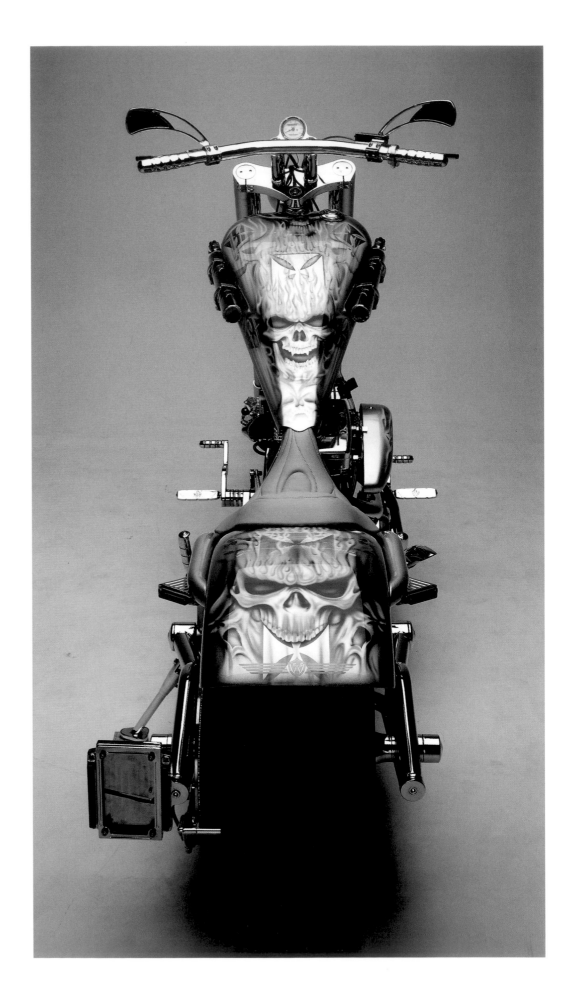

Retro Chopper

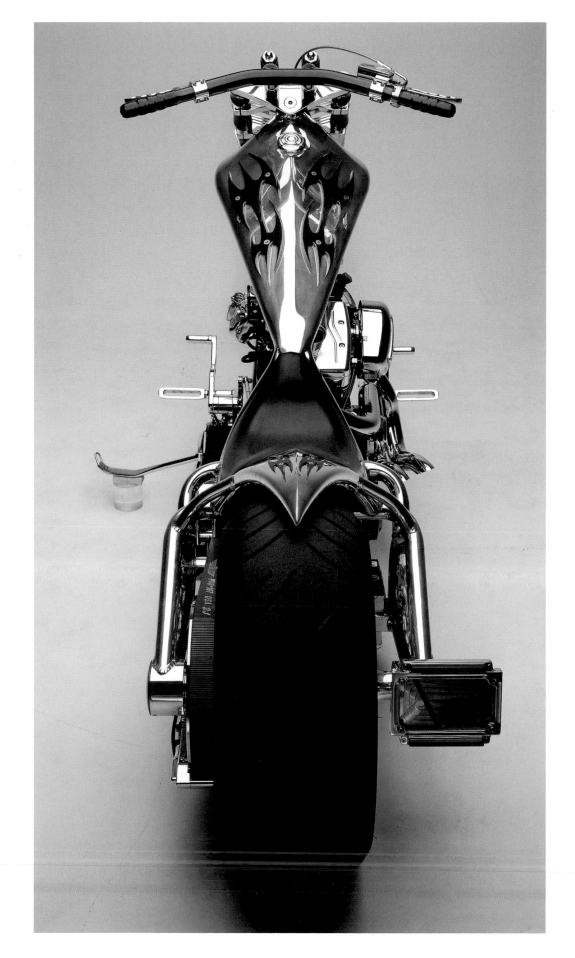

ART CENTER COLLEGE OF DESIGN LIBRARY

Chapter 3

Chica

Old School Cool

The police in Huntington Beach, California, don't like loud motorcycles. In fact, they don't appreciate custom motorcycles at all. Modifications that violate the stringently enforced vehicle codes can get your bike the hook. The police must keep busy, considering that this community is home to Yasuyoshi Chikazawa, "Chica" as he is known throughout the world, builder of some of the most strident choppers in America.

Like a Japanese James Dean, Chica cultivates 1950s style, right down to the pompadour haircut, turned-up collar, and ever-present cigarette dangling from his lips. The ambient music surrounding his shop leans toward punk, the only incongruity with the time-period flavor.

When a friend let teenaged Chica ride his motorcycle in Osaka, Japan, he became hooked on the sport almost immediately. He began to devour past issues of *Easyriders* magazine whenever he could get his hands on copies from America. The early Arlen Ness bikes were a big influence on Chica. Eventually, Chica acquired a used Harley-Davidson FXE, the cheapest Big-Twin Harley available in Japan at the time, but he had his heart set on a Low Rider. "To me, at the time, it was the name, shape, and style that was totally different than any other Harley." Harley parts were prohibitively expensive in Japan. So was mechanical labor. You either had to be rich or willing to learn how to work on your own bike to keep a Harley running. You also had to learn how to fix and fabricate parts. Chica supported his Harley habit by working as a mechanic in a Honda dealership.

In 1990, Chica left the Honda shop and went to work for an independent Harley dealer in Kyoto. He stayed there for two years before deciding he was ready to open his own shop.

He was already dreaming about coming to America by this time. Friends told him that in the U.S.A. people could do whatever they wanted with motorcycles. There were no rules! But in Japan he couldn't vent his imagination because the prices of parts were double and sometimes triple what they were in the States. In 1997, Chica accepted a job offer from a motorcycle shop in California. Soon after he arrived in the promised land of milk and motor oil, he began building his own custom motorcycles.

Although he has been living in the United States for six years, Chica's English vocabulary doesn't extend far beyond colloquialisms and the names of motorcycle parts. Chica's choppers do most of his speaking for him. With the help of his crew, he builds choppers as if time has stood still since the 1950s. It seems as though Chica and his crew started from scratch and have not been effected by the exaggerated influences of choppers from the 1960s and 1970s. They've picked up where the bobbers left off, as if they were laying their own groundwork for the evolution of choppers. In their minds, the "Golden Age of Choppers" hasn't happened yet. They will invent their own.

When asked if his business has been hurt by an adverse economy, Chica replied, "Any business at all is a plus." He will always keep

that mental outlook because, "I didn't start out with zero; I started out with zero *minus*."

Chica has an unusual building style. He doesn't use a lift; he doesn't even own one. After preliminary sketches are completed and all of the parts are available, they are arranged around the frame on the floor in his small, somewhat cluttered garage.

What appeals most to Chica about motorcycles are the motors. When asked why, he replies, "Cool as hell!" Chica considers the engine the most essential, artistic aspect of a motorcycle. Chica works almost exclusively with classic motors and doesn't use reproductions, only the real deals. He hardly knows what to do with a modern motor—they don't speak to him. The character of an engine suggests to him the creative direction to follow. Older engines deliver less power with smaller displacements, but they retain a certain character that is lacking in modern motors.

Chica builds bikes that come from within his personal experience of life. His choppers are wonderful contradictions. They're fast, clean, and cool, but in a retrograde grunge kind of way. People have told Chica that his bikes are too scary looking. But he tells them that if they ride one, they won't be able to let go. He asks rhetorically why people want to ride custom motorcycles in the first place. His answer: "It's not for touring. It's not to commute to work. The bottom line is that riding a custom bike is lots of fun."

Chica puts his heart and soul into every motorcycle and is grateful for those who praise him for his work. Every time he builds a bike for himself to ride, someone wants to buy it. Since he has to make a living, it's hard to refuse a decent offer. Usually, the only bike he owns at any given time lies in parts. But Chica says he is always flattered—"most happy" in fact—when a bike he built for himself, one reflecting his own persona, is coveted by someone who is probably not like him at all. It means they want to possess a part of him.

Chica has built only about 30 bikes so far, making them quite rare. He wouldn't discourage their display in a museum as works of art, if that should ever happen, but he would rather see them ridden. As other builders will agree, riding is also the art of the chopper.

The parts of a great motorcycle are at the disposal of anyone who wants to build one. The essential ingredients remain the same for everyone: wheels, brakes, motor, and transmission. They all look pretty much the same too. But according to Chica, what distinguishes a *great* motorcycle—a work of art versus an ordinary motorcycle—is *balance*. "Balance in a custom motorcycle. . . . I think of it the same as balance in a person's face or body." Symmetry, grace, uniqueness, beauty: Balance.

Rumbler

Untitled

Von Dutch

Untitled

Chapter 4

Jerry Covington

Big Man in Town

ONE MIGHT NOT EXPECT TO FIND A PLACE LIKE COVINGTON'S CYCLE CITY in Woodward, a small, windswept town in the northwest corner of Oklahoma. Nevertheless, it presides over Woodward's main drag as a shrine to that most urban of fire-belching street machines: the chopper. Since Jerry Covington opened his shop in 1993, many disciples of great motorcycles have made the pilgrimage to Woodward.

Covington loves to build choppers, a genre of motorcycle he sums up in three words: "Less is more. You take everything off you don't need, and just leave what it takes to go down the road."

"I started building choppers in the early seventies," recalls Jerry Covington. "My first bikes had to have long [tall] springers and had to have rigid frames. I thought that was the only chopper there was. I used to go over to Denver's Choppers [in Riverside] and hang out. Somehow or another, that's the chopper shop I got hooked up with. They were also doing what they called San Francisco low riders at the time, which was the real low, real stretched bikes. That's the choppers I remember."

When Covington was 16, he traded a hot rod car for his first used Harley. By the time he was 18, he had built his first chopper. It was black with lots of chrome and a springer front end on a rigid frame. It was also his first wreck.

On his way to work one morning, he was riding along a street when a woman fifty years his senior opted to make a left turn across traffic and collided with Jerry just about head on. He broke both of his hips and was laid up in traction for three and a half months.

While he was lying in the hospital, he thought about the insurance money he would collect for his bike. When he was released from the hospital, he went down to the local Harley-Davidson dealer—*still on crutches!*— and bought a brand-new, stock 1977 Super Glide. He soon became bored with it and traded it for an older used bike that formed the basis of his next chopper.

He began building custom cars for a living, but built a bike every now and again to keep his chopper jones appeased. By 1992, he'd had enough of California and moved his operation to Oklahoma. Jerry intended to continue building custom cars there, but got sidetracked. He built himself a new chopper to ride, but no sooner had the sun first shone off on its chrome than someone offered to buy it. That quickly became routine. He began building one bike after another. A year went by, and after witnessing the fabulous growth of the bike business, he decided to make building choppers his business instead of his hobby. That led to the founding of Covington's Cycle City.

"If I wasn't going to build my own chopper, if I had to buy one from somebody else, I would say right of the top of my head, Eddie Trotta. Our styles are definitely different; you can tell one from the other. But we've got a lot of the same ideas."

About his own ideas, his own expression of the art of the chopper, Covington won't hang metal on a chassis just to cover some otherwise unsightly detail. Jerry believes that

every detail of construction and fabrication counts, whether it is readily visible or not. "I like the bottom side of my bike to look as good as the top side of my bike. I don't care if you pull the battery up or pull the seat up, what's underneath should be detailed, too." He wants people to see the craftsmanship that goes into his motorcycles.

Covington pays close attention to the flowing lines of a chopper from front to back. "You won't have a tank kicked up too much in the front so the bike looks broken," he says. "We won't throw parts on that don't look like they belong." If he executes a diamond-shape theme or a spade-shape theme somewhere on the bike, that theme will be employed throughout the design. No part is used gratuitously.

When asked if he considers himself an artist, Covington replies, "Definitely yes. Just like a picture is created, drawn, and colored in and all that, to me it's the same, except we do ours in metal. If every motorcycle wasn't a piece of art, it wouldn't matter what they looked like."

But just because he considers his choppers works of art doesn't mean Covington is averse to riding them hard. "There's a difference between abusing [a chopper] and riding it hard," Jerry says. Covington's bikes are built to be ridden. He won't build a bike just for show. "You might as well just take a picture of a bike if you're going to make it where you can't ride it."

Covington builds some, but not all, bikes with 124-cubic-inch motors. "You can have a big, rideable, manageable motor, as long as you don't get too out of control," he says. "They make more power as you turn them up hard, but if you're cruising around on them they're fine. I think you could ride some distance with those. Everybody's got to have big numbers. Honestly, they probably don't use 80% percent of their motor. It's just the fact that they've got it [the power] there when they want it. A small motor nowadays is a 107 [cubic inch]."

Jerry Covington's great joy is watching customers walk out of his shop to sit for the first time on their new chopper. "These guys are strutting." But Cycle City has seen some interesting customers take delivery of motorcycles. "Some people get on them, you really hold your breath," says Covington. One fellow came to pick up his new bike. It hadn't ever been ridden before. The motor wasn't broken in. The guy jumped on and made five passes in front of the shop at 80 miles per hour in a 40 miles per hour zone. "Where are the police?" wondered Jerry. "They're usually all over the place." He gave the guy his pink slip and off he went. Jerry knew that that bike and motor were going to suffer serious abuse. "Oh, yeah. It hurts. I just don't want to see it again and try to fix it."

As for the chopper's place in the grand scheme of motorcycle culture, Jerry says, "Some of us will never stop riding [choppers]. I don't think they'll ever go away. Not completely. I had a guy tell me years ago, if you do custom—*true* custom—you'll always have something to do, because the guy who has everything doesn't want something he can walk in an buy."

As far as Covington is concerned, it can't be a custom bike—choppers notwithstanding—unless it has some custom fabrication. "Something has to separate a custom bike from a bolt-together. Oh yeah, it's got to be something more than a paint job,"

Untitled

Untitled

Untitled

Untitled

Art Center College of Design
Library
1700 Lida Street
Pasadena, Calif. 91103

Chapter 5

Matt Hotch

Mr. Clean

ONE OF THE MOTORCYCLE INDUSTRY'S FOREMOST INNOVATORS, Matt Hotch is responsible for some of the most sublime custom choppers on the planet. His dark, intellectually engaging eyes reflect the convergence of his Czech and Vietnamese heritage. Straight black hair hangs in a ponytail below his waist, and true to his generation, he sports a nose ring, though his soft-spoken dialogue is seldom punctuated by gratuitous expletives. He admits to chugging a few bottles of Miller High Life on occasion, but he favors Coca-Cola. He has quit smoking cigarettes, but once had a four-pack-per-day habit.

Matt doesn't even have a motorcycle of his own. "If I spend too much time riding," he laments, "it's all over. There goes the business!" At least he can hop on any one of his latest creations at a moment's notice for a shakedown scoot. To give a new bike its final stamp of approval, Matt rides it home to show his wife.

Matt's mother often visits him at work. She is "Mama Hotch" to everyone in the shop, but Twee is her Vietnamese name. A diminutive woman with a strong presence, Mama Hotch enjoys photographing her son's bikes.

Hotch declines to participate in television extravaganzas such as the self-styled "build-offs" featured on cable channels, and he doesn't follow the promotional circuit to places such as Sturgis or Daytona Beach. He thinks the costs are too high. Television producers don't reimburse builders for parts and assembly time up-front, and personal appearances distract him from the hands-on labor he dedicates to making motorcycles. He attends only industry trade shows to display his signature Hot Match™ handlebars, gas caps, kickstands, and radial pipes, for distributors.

When it comes down to his approach as a builder, Matt Hotch is Mr. Clean, but that doesn't mean his work is sterile; it seethes with infectious style. Cleanliness refers to his state-of-the-art assemblies, such as switches, wiring, and cables that Hotch routes everywhere but where you can see them. If you look closely at a Hot Match chopper, you might doubt it will even run because it's so hard to see the spaghetti. For example, Matt's signature ignition switch is pathologically inconspicuous. It is hidden under the seat, but you don't have to lift the seat to start the engine. You just have to know where to press your thumb.

While even the most tricked-out Hot Match bikes are built to be ridden hard, an unfamiliar mechanic might have difficulty finding—let alone reaching—a brake line for routine maintenance. One bike has the most complex rear-view mirror ever seen on a motorcycle. A tiny rearward-facing digital camera is mounted on the swing arm adjacent to the rear axle. Wires from the camera run through the frame to a small LCD screen mounted flush into the gas tank. "Customers who want to ride those bikes are married to me for life," Matt says.

According to Hotch, "A chopper is basically a motorcycle that has been customized to reflect its owner's self image." Matt builds them in many different ways. "I'm very fortunate to be able to build a bike in my head. My engineering skills are self-taught. When I want to run a wire or a cable, I *imagine* exactly where it has to go. If I drill a hole, it won't kink the line. It's not an afterthought.

"Bike builders are a dime a dozen nowadays," admonishes Matt. "But one thing that separates the top builders from the rest is that they're not just taking someone else's design and tweaking it a little bit. They're the innovative ones. You *can* build a bike from a catalog. I actually did it myself. I built a giveaway bike for J&P [from parts in their catalog]." His yellow-and-blue chopper with ape hangers is featured on the cover of J&P's 2003 catalog. It looks very cool, but doesn't look anything like a Hot Match signature model. Matt says, "People who excel in building custom motorcycles are artists. We're able to see motorcycles differently. It's not just a machine. It has a personal effect on us."

Matt doesn't want his business to get to a point where he has to hire employees to build bikes because that's what *he* likes to do. His customers come to him because they know he'll personally build their Hot Match custom choppers. Hot Match has employees, but none of them work in the shop. "Nobody else touches it except for me," Matt insists.

If Matt Hotch wasn't a builder and wanted to buy a custom chopper, he would choose Billy Lane to build it. Billy's homespun-but-hip ingenuity reminds him of the seat-of-your-pants learning curve he endured while starting out building bikes in his father's garage. Arlen Ness was Matt's earliest inspiration, though. He acknowledges Ness as the king, and proudly says, "Now my parts are featured in his [Ness'] catalog. He looks at me as a peer. The people I idolized now respect my own work."

Born in Minneapolis, Minnesota, in 1974, Matt's family moved to Fullerton in Orange County, California, when he was 10 years old. By the time he was 12 years old, Matt was working on cars in the family garage. When he was 16, he bartered a rebuilt VW for his first Harley. Soon, friends brought him bikes to work on, mostly basket cases. That was the start of his career. Matt says with amusement, "I learned by screwing up everybody else's bike!"

Matt is a quick study as well as a determined one, but he didn't do well in school. In fact, Matt was expelled from high school and had to graduate from a continuation academy. Matt won't say specifically what got him the boot, but he confesses that he didn't react well to authority. Everyone close to him is glad he finally found his niche.

Because Matt does all the sheet-metal work, it can take as long as one and one-half year to ride home on a Hot Match chopper after you plunk down a deposit. Matt doesn't like to disappoint clients by giving them false deadlines, but he tries to get the job done in six or eight months. He works hard to make everybody happy.

II Feat

Untitled

Amarillo

ART CENTER COLLEGE OF DESIGN LIBRARY

Continental

Cuerito

Gold Member

Chapter 6

Cyril Huze

The Romance of Riding

THOUGH CONTRADICTORY OPINIONS CONCERNING WHAT A CHOPPER IS ABOUND, Cyril Huze says, "I would say that everybody knows what *is not* a chopper." One traditional definition is that all parts not necessary to make a motorcycle faster are removed, altering the motorcycle's cosmetic appearance, or *cosmetique* as Huze describes it. Though popular wisdom supports this theory, Huze believes that the current popularity of the genre has more to do with our attempts at defining who we are. "It is a rebellion because you take a factory object and transform it to make it *yours* and to make a statement." He believes it's not the way a bike looks that makes it a chopper; it's something you feel when you look at the bike.

"The main characteristic remaining of the choppers, the common characteristic of the seventies and today, would be the long front end," Huze continues. "Today, because of the creativity of builders, you can still have the chopper attitude without respect to the traditional geometry of the seventies."

Huze credits the baby-boomer generation's infatuation with Harley-Davidson motorcycles with the current resurgence in the popularity of choppers. When the number of conventional-looking bikes on the road reached critical mass, there was a backlash from long-time traditional bikers. Everyone looks alike on a bike, at least on a conventional Harley-Davidson. Now that municipal court judges, doctors, airline pilots, plumbers, school teachers, and truckers are all riding together and wearing the same costumes, they have achieved much of what they set out to do: escape from the monotony and routine of their stations in life through play acting.

But the guys who have been riding all along, who subscribe to their own alternative lifestyle, are not happy about rubbing shoulders with the mainstream of society. Like these long-time bikers, younger riders want to differentiate themselves from their parents riding baggers and billet barges. Both camps have made a conscious decision to return to the roots of motorcycling.

"My inspiration is art," says Huze, describing his approach to building bikes. Like an artist, he always begins a project with sketches before he starts to build. He covers all views: front, back, three-quarter rear, three-quarter front. He doesn't like to improvise. He never starts a motorcycle until he has a theme to work with. "My job is to write the storyboard of the motorcycle," says Cyril, speaking as if he were a movie producer. "For me, creativity is to make two parts that have never met look good together."

When Huze was 21 years old and still living in his native city of Paris, France, he bought his first motorcycle, a blue FLH Electra Glide, and has been riding ever since. Huze fell in love with motorcycles in the most ardently passionate European manner and became determined to make motorcycles look and behave the way he always imagined they should. In 1992 Huze decided to chuck a successful advertising career that had brought him to New York City and follow his childhood dream of building custom motorcycles. He set up shop in Boca Raton, Florida.

The most embarrassing moment of Cyril's motorcycle career occurred before he turned pro. He had customized his own motorcycle and entered it in a competition sponsored by Harley-Davidson at Sturgis in 1992. To his surprise, Cyril was the winner. When it came time for his victory lap around the audience, his bike wouldn't start. He was ready to push it after too many humiliating failed attempts, but Willie G. Davidson, who was one of the judges, suggested he try just one more time. Success! He received a huge ovation. It may have been an embarrassing moment, but it encouraged his nascent career.

When he receives a new commission, Cyril will spend a couple of days with his client. He wants to hear the music they listen to, meet their wives or girlfriends, know what movies they like to see, and which books they like to read. He wants to see how they dress, decorate their homes; the color of their bath towels. Huze has twelve points outlined on his Web site that, in his mind, represent a philosophy for building custom motorcycles. The final one is: "A good designer is not the one who takes you from what you have to what you want, but the one who takes you from what you want to what you didn't even know you wanted."

If Huze wanted to buy a chopper, he'd pay a visit to Billy Lane. Lane's work is different from his own, but Huze appreciates his innovative talent and the fresh approach he brings to the industry. "I think the artistry in this business comes not only from the creative competition between professional builders," says Cyril Huze about the *crème de la crème* of customizers, "but also from individuals in their garages who bring a lot of new ideas [to the forefront]. When you go to bike shows, you are going always to see individuals [amateurs], not professionals—it can be their first bike, sometimes second bike, third bike—who come with amazing things that nobody in the industry ever thought of before. And we are inspired by these people. I respect them a lot.

"I'm very romantic about motorcycles," says Cyril. "There's a lot of romance in riding." He still loves to ride. Each year, Huze makes a long road trip with friends. He'll ride for ten days at a time ideally across the vast expanses of the American West. "It's the most American landscape," Huze says. "In Europe, we have stereotypes about America. It can be the landscape, the American natives, Kennedy, James Dean….

"And one of the stereotypes is Harley-Davidson. No matter what we builders say— even 'Fuck the Factory' you see on T–shirts—we all started because of Harley-Davidson. The American cop on a Harley-Davison is an image I had in my mind as a child. I played with a toy cop on a Harley-Davidson." When Huze first set foot on U.S. soil in Chicago as a tourist in 1978, the first thing he noticed during his taxi ride downtown was a cop wearing a blue helmet, sitting on a Harley, chewing gum. The cop looked just like Huze's toy come alive. It was an emotional experience for the 25-year-old Cyril. He felt like he was in a movie. In many ways, his life still has a certain cinematic quality. Unlike many of the classic biker films of the 1960s, Huze's personal movie appears to be heading towards a happy ending.

Surreal Huze

ART CENTER COLLEGE OF DESIGN LIBRARY

Untitled

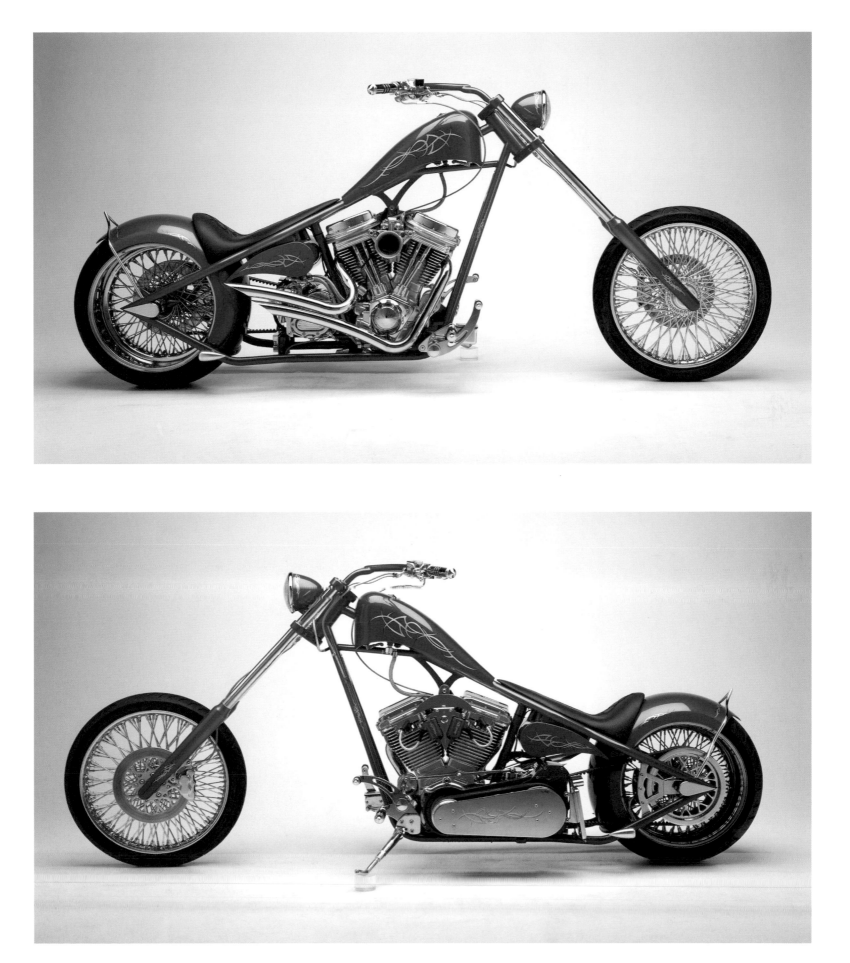

Chapter 7

Pat Kennedy

The Real Deal

PAT KENNEDY IS A BIKER, THE REAL DEAL. He defines *chopper* with one word: *life*. "There is no other feeling," he says. "There is no other motorcycle. This is a true center."

"I don't want it to escape me," says Kennedy about the state of being he achieves aboard a chopper. "And I don't want to share it. It's not a group thing. I don't ride in any groups."

Pat Kennedy's workshop, a restored barn, dates back to Arizona Territory times. Each bay, formerly a horse stall, is organized by a particular task: one for bending frames, one for welding, one for forming sheet metal, one for motor assembly, one for paint, and so on. "It has a different world in every stall," Pat says.

Motorcycling is in Kennedy's genes; his two older brothers rode. From the time he could turn a wrench, he was working on motorcycles in the family garage. By the time he was 12 years old, Pat was riding his brothers' bikes. Pat says that his brothers' rule of thumb was, "When I could start it, pick it up [off the kick stand], and turn the front end I could ride it." This was tricky because these were long choppers, and nobody knew about rake and trail geometry in those days. "The front wheel was heavier than hell," Pat recalls. "And this was kick-start only. There were no buttons to be pushed." He uses electric starters today. "These knees have seen better days."

By the time Kennedy was in the sixth grade, he had already built his first bike for a paying customer, the president of a local bike club. By the time he was 15, he had enough money to buy his own scoot and chop it. He found a Sportster that belonged to crazed druggie from San Francisco who had already sold the front end for a fix. Pat picked up the rest of the bike for $1,000, mounted a springer front end, then stretched the frame and laid on some purple flames. "I rode the pee out of it," Pat says.

Kennedy's education is well rounded. He has been certified by the state of California as machinist and a welder. He has associate degrees in auto body and automotive frame straightening. And he has a college degree in law enforcement. That little pirouette in the course of his career was, as he says, "a necessity of life." At one point, Pat figured he was spending 30 percent of his time dealing with the law as an outsider, if not quite an outlaw. Even though he didn't use alcohol or other drugs or engage in any criminal activity, the authorities branded him as part of the criminal element simply because he rode choppers. After much harassment he decided to gain some insider insight to deal with these intrusions.

"I have a specific look that I think is 'a biker.' And it looks like me. I don't mean breaking the law, doing drugs, or being a fucking idiot. A biker isn't trying to be the center of attention; he's just doing what he's doing." Pat wears nobody's colors, no patches. He is a club of one. At one time back in California, Pat was placed under police surveillance for one year. He caught detectives sifting through his trash. One particular cop was assigned to park his cruiser in front of Pat's shop during business hours every day. He was sold a bill of goods and was predisposed to hate Pat's guts. Pat would exasperate him by knocking on his car window every day trying to start a conversation. After a while the cop relented. Within six months, the two became friends. "He was a bro'," Kennedy says.

After moving his operation to Arizona, a biker-friendly cop informed Kennedy that he had been the subject of the largest investigation conducted since the territory became a state. He had moved into a small town and built an eight-foot-high fence around his property with cameras mounted on the gates. Soon, visitors were flying their jets in and out of the community airport. He doesn't blame the local authorities for responding to the alarms going off in their minds: Drug dealer! How were they to know that the hubbub was about motorcycles, not methamphetamines?

"Many things are fun at the level you don't *have* to do them," Kennedy says about his chosen career. Pat builds motorcycles because he loves to do it, not because he is compelled to grow a business. If no one was willing to buy his motorcycles, he'd build them anyway. Nevertheless, business has been good for him.

Kennedy doesn't spend much time looking at magazines because he doesn't want too much outside influence on his work. But even he can't avoid seeing a motorcycle occasionally and gasping, "Whoa! Why didn't I do that? Look how this works!" Part of

Kennedy's philosophy dictates that every part on a motorcycle must have a dual purpose: 1) It has to perform its nominal function; and 2) it has to look good doing it. In his mind, form and function must contribute equally to pull the weight of a chopper, both literally and figuratively.

It has to be long. It has to have a radical rake, too. "A chopper to me is a massive motorcycle. If I look back at my roots, at growing up and seeing all these bikes running in southern California, the size of them was what I considered normal."

It used to be that if you saw a long bike on the road, you could take for granted that it was one of his creations. He was making custom, high end, over-the-top chops when few if any other builders were doing so. There has been no renaissance in the art of the chopper for Pat Kennedy. He's been making them the same way all along.

Kennedy says, "I've never built a motorcycle in my life that I haven't bled on." His hands have the scars to prove it. He can look at this scar and remember one bike, look at that scar and visualize another bike. Pat thinks anybody can build a custom bike from catalog parts, with *his* parts or anybody else's. But as he says, "It's not a Pat Kennedy bike." It's easy enough to determine if a bike is an original Kennedy chopper because he signs each motorcycle he makes. So no matter if all the parts came from Kennedy's shop, it's not a Pat Kennedy original unless he fabricated the whole shebang and put it together himself. He has to bleed on it.

Is Pat Kennedy an artist? "I don't know. Art is a tough word," he replies. "I would consider myself a craftsman." He signs his work, he says, because he wants people to know where it came from. "There have been many imitators. I want you to know it's real, and what it's meant." Then, after a long deliberative pause, "No, not art." Just a chopper? "Yeah."

Easy Rider

Chapter 8

Billy Lane

Riding the Sex Machine

BILLY LANE ADMITS TO BUILDING BIKES THAT ARE BEAUTIFUL, "BUT NEVER PRETTY." Ladled with an East Coast-city "sauce" and served raw, they project speed, power, and, most of all, respect.

Found objects often make their way into his *bike tartare* recipe. And for that, Billy is as much a warm-hearted romantic as he is a stone-cold biker. "I might see an old water faucet that is 60 or 70 years old," he says. "I wonder how many people have used it and where?" Including something funky for effect that has obviously endured time bestows a certain kind of charm upon his motorcycles. Billy blends kitsch with chic in an oddball sort of way. No one else could get away with a porcelain toilet handle for a petcock.

Billy marvels at vintage bikes and wonders how many dirt roads they've bounced along; how many maniacs—ghosts now—rode them from one adventure to the next throughout earlier generations. "An old bike has a real, certain mystique to it." He likes to sprinkle some of that mystique, some vintage ingredients, onto his new bikes.

Born in Miami on February 6, 1970, Billy is barely old enough to remember the first wave of chopper popularity. As a child, Billy heard and saw them constantly around south Florida. He remembers one afternoon with his brother and mother when he excitedly pointed out a large bunch of tattooed bikers approaching them from up the street. His exasperated mother yelled at him above the roar of their pipes, "Don't look, don't look!"

His older brother put him on a bike for the first time at the age of 18 and rekindled his interest in choppers. By then, nobody but a bunch of diehards and throwbacks wanted to be seen on one. Billy found a 1950 Panhead in pieces. Through trial and error he put

it together and made it run. Once it was on the street, that old bike was cool enough to catch the attention of some hardcore club guys down in south Florida. They took a shine to the wet-behind-the-ears college kid with short hair and no tattoos. "By being me, I've always been different," Billy says. Those old-school one-percenters invited him to hang out at the clubhouse and drink beer. They taught him a lot about maintaining his motorcycle.

After earning a degree in mechanical engineering, Billy moved back to Miami to work in his brother's motorcycle shop. There he combined his mechanical aptitude with a penchant for putting the right—or wrong—pieces together in just the right way, as a sculptor would, to make motorcycles that became more than the sums of their parts. By early 1995, he had already begun to establish himself independently.

During those early years Billy couldn't afford to buy new engines, so he bought old machines and rebuilt them. He still does this, but not because he has to. He's grown fond of old iron, believing older engines have more character. "You can see where the moving parts are," he says. Watching form follow function puts him under a spell.

While contemplating an aged flathead, Knuckle, or Shovel, he might see a road map of scars on a grizzled face or the puffy mien of a boxer with his nose out of joint. Those old mills represent a cast of tough guys from a 1940s vintage, black-and-white film noir. Each one tells him a different story and helps him outline a plot for the next bike he builds.

Once a chopper is finished, he makes it part of himself simply by riding it. To Billy, riding a chopper is a privilege, a badge of honor, to be earned. Regarding his philosophy of riding a chopper, Billy says, "There's very little to work with, but you learn how to deal with what you've got. It takes moxie." Billy really does ride his choppers like he stole them. They're not coddled just because they were once on the cover of some biker rag. Billy puts every bike he builds through its paces on a regular basis. They *look* rode hard and put away wet. To Billy, hard riding demonstrates respect for a motorcycle.

Typically, Billy rides every day. Unless it is absolutely pouring rain—maybe even if it is—he rides his bikes to work. If a customer's bike is in the shop for any reason and Billy wants to ride it, he'll ride it. He won't work with customers who aren't cool with that. He likes to make sure the machines are always in top mechanical order, and riding them helps him keep a feel for their tuned performance. Billy rides each bike he builds long enough to learn its every idiosyncrasy before he turns over the keys to its new owner. "It's kind of like sleeping with a woman," he says. "You learn what they like, how they feel, and you learn everything else about them. And then you move on to the next one!

"Every element I need to be happy is right there when I'm riding," he claims. If there's time to ride cross-country from Florida to California, that's what he'll do to make his appointment. The television program *Biker Build-Offs*, in which Billy is featured, has afforded him a little extra time to promote his career and have some great fun riding at the same time.

Until he built his recent Camel bike, *Blue Suicide* was Billy's favorite bike. It's perhaps the one he has ridden most often for the past two years. It's been totaled and rebuilt twice. When asked how he got it back after it was once stolen, Billy replies, "I'm connected. [What happened to the thief is] something you ain't gonna put in your book!"

In addition to building his highly acclaimed choppers, Billy likes to surf. He keeps himself occupied in his spare time with weightlifting and kick boxing. Working hard doesn't make Billy a dull boy. He likes to play pool and drink beer. He slices off as much life as he can chew. Billy is a party biker, no doubt about it. Billy believes he has everything he has ever wanted out of life, and that if he were to check out tomorrow, he'd ride off into the sunset a happy man.

By Billy's standards a chopper is minimalistic. It is handmade and exhibits human qualities, just short of perfection.

Jerry's Bike

Psycho Billy Cadillac

Knuckle Sandwich

Art Center College of Design
Library
1700 Lida Street
Pasadena, Calif. 91103

Camel Bike

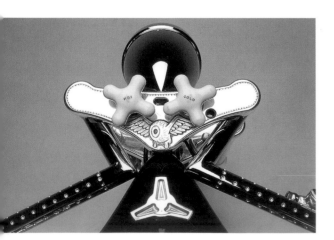

Chapter 9

Martin Brothers

Tuning Up the Motorcycle Business

THE BOND BETWEEN BROTHERS JOE AND JASON MARTIN EXTENDS BEYOND FAMILY. They are deeply committed friends and business partners. In spite of spending just about every day of their lives together, they still enjoy each other's company.

The brothers dreamt of a musical career when they were young. Motorcycles gained precedence over music for the practical purpose of creating revenue, but building choppers provides a means for the brothers to satisfy their artistic urges. Joe explains, "If I had a bad night playing, you know, my phrasing was bad, my timing was bad, or my amp sounded like crap in a room with bad acoustics, it would bum me out for days. With the bike thing, I can just go back there [in the shop] and tweak it a little bit and fix it [if something goes wrong]."

Jason has a more practical take on the difference between the two art forms. He jokes, "Building bikes, you don't have to work with a damned band! Musicians are flakes, man."

As a child, Joe remembers seeing choppers on the streets of Carbondale, Illinois. "Back in the late 1970s before choppers were cool, you'd see guys riding around on these old greasy, raggedy Shovelheads and Panheads with jockey shifts. They seemed real taboo." Joe recollects.

After the family moved to Dallas, Jason became fascinated by a chopped Knucklehead parked in the garage of the apartment building where the Martin family lived. That bike was forbidden fruit to a naïve kid. Anybody who owned a Harley in those days, Jason recounts, must have been "an ass-kicker." Harleys weren't a common sight. "I thought I could get in trouble just looking at it."

Shortly after Joe's graduation, the boys' mother got a job out of state. Jason had one more year of high school. Neither Joe nor Jason wanted to leave Dallas, so the two teenage brothers lived without parental supervision.

To finance their musical ambitions, Jason worked two jobs and Joe worked at a place called Super Shops busting tires and installing cams for local hot rodders. He learned to paint and stripe by studying the illustrations he found in magazines.

The brothers eased their way into the customization business. Their first paint shop, so to speak, was in the kitchen of a house they rented. "We used to scrap on just the shittiest cars you can imagine," says Jason. "I was Joe's painter-helper." Jason would decorate the kitchen with car hoods, side panels, fenders, and doors. These were canvases for Joe's airbrushed graphics. It was a crazy scene with dogs running around barking and loud music playing all the time. There were people everywhere, constantly coming and going.

By this time, Joe and Jason were well connected with the Dallas custom car scene, but they had had no involvement with motorcycles. Gradually, as one acquaintance after another brought Joe a used Harley for new paint, word got around to the local bike shops that his work was superior.

Joe bought a 1951 Panhead. Soon afterward, Jason found a Shovelhead for himself. "The first thing we did was shred them," as Jason tells it. They didn't always keep track of how things fit back together though. They eventually figured things out.

They worked on bikes in the living room because the garage was occupied by Joe's cars. All of their furniture got scrunched into the dining room. Then they bought an outdoor, prefabricated shed; installed a small exhaust fan and a space heater; and turned it into a paint booth when the quantity of work outgrew the kitchen.

The Martin brothers have very definite ideas when it comes to the art of the chopper. "Every part of a bike is art. Every part of it has to look right. Everything shows," Jason says. Starting from scratch with a motorcycle, he knows that he can pull something from inside himself, something that no one has ever seen before.

Jason believes that choppers should not necessarily be comfortable. The "stance" of a bike, as he puts it, and the rider's posture while on it are primary aspects of this art. It's certainly not about transportation. "It would look goofy to have a set of really comfortable bars, like a set of stock buckhorns [on a chopper]."

More important to the Martins' customers than comfort, according to Joe, is that "they want to look cool, and they want to carry a passenger 'cause they want to get laid."

"A chopper should tell you something about the person who's going to ride it," says Jason. Joe agrees and adds that there is a "chopper spirit" that guides his hand when he creates motorcycles.

Jason Martin admires Billy Lane's old-school ethic. "Billy's stuff is cool because it's almost like he's making fun of the whole thing," reasons Joe. Matt Hotch is also admired by both brothers for his "ultimately clean" bikes and his sleek "sanitary" designs.

Neither Joe nor Jason gets to ride as much as they wish. When it's wet they don't ride, and they just endured an unusually wet winter. Even during the spring, a downpour can unexpectedly develop into a fearsome hailstorm and pelt hapless riders with golf ball to grapefruit sized rocks of ice than can kill a cow. Add a heavy professional workload and their musical sideline to the exigencies of the weather and the Martin brothers barely find time to ride at all.

"Building bikes doesn't make us a penny," says Jason. Their company earns most of its income from the exhaust pipes it sells. "By the time you're finished building a bike for $15,000 in parts, you think you can sell it for $30,000 and make money. What the hell? No way. By the time you're done with it dude…"

Joe chimes in, "Yeah, that's five bucks an hour!" They both laugh again.

"You don't want to think about logical shit when you're building a bike," Jason says.

Joe has one beef with the recent spike in chopper popularity. He sees irony in the fact that growing business for the Martin Brothers and others has led to a crass commercialization of the chopper esthetic.

"They're kind of taking the cool out of them; you know what I mean?" he complains.

When Joe and Jason were asked if they knew any young builders who hadn't yet found their "fifteen minutes of fame" they quickly replied in unison: "Us!" They were laughing. They're well on their way.

Purple Gangsta

Trend Killer

Untitled

Untitled

Chapter 10

Russell Mitchell

Exile on Mainstream

"I HAVE A HARD TIME WITH FITTING OVER-FENDERED, Softail-framed bikes with heavy gas tanks into the chopper genre," says Russell Mitchell with the pleasantly drawn-out vowels of a British expatriate. "There are some Softail choppers out there that have been done real clean and can look almost rigid; and we do them occasionally for customers. But I don't think there's any real definition. I don't think it really matters. It's a *bike*. I consider pretty much everything we do to be a chopper, even the short stubby bikes."

Mitchell developed an interest in motorcycles while still living in his native city of London, England. He says motorcycling appealed to him initially because it was an efficient way to piss off his parents. "They maintain a lot of that Victorian mentality. It's all about what the neighbors think. At 21, I was thinking about my first tattoo. Instead of sitting me down and saying 'think about it, son, it could hold you back in life,' they left a message saying I'd be cut out of the will. You can't talk to a 21 year old like that. I was on my bike at 100 miles per hour to the tattoo shop that day."

The scope of Mitchell's motorcycle fixation soon grew to include building custom bikes as well as riding them. "If I had the money to build the 'baddest' custom in England, I would. If I didn't, it would be a flat-black, Jap four.

"This was the late eighties. The economy sucked in England. The weather *always* sucks in England. And I had probably the best-paying veterinarian job out of anyone I went through university with. I had a side gig modeling for one of the best agencies in London, and I was still driving around in a car the size of a matchbox, living in a two bedroom flat in a shitty part of London, and just about able to keep a Jap bike on the road."

Russell traveled to Los Angeles on vacation to visit a girlfriend, a model who had come to America to work for six months. She hooked him up with her agent who asked Mitchell to come out to Los Angeles and work as a model. In 1991 Mitchell left London and moved to the Los Angeles area.

In L.A., any sort of modeling gig quickly turns into some kind of acting opportunity, and that's what happened to Russell. He eked out a living as an actor, but he knew he was never going to be a Brad Pitt. After wrapping up a Marlboro commercial that put a little bit of money in his bank account, Mitchell succumbed to his old habits and built a couple of custom bikes for a friend. "I really got carried away on those," he remembers. They got a lot of attention and there were numerous offers to buy some of the parts he had designed. Mitchell thought to himself, "I'm a struggling actor with nothing but free time, and I need nothing more than a bit of supplementary income."

Within a few months, part-time motorcycle building became Mitchell's full-time occupation. Exile Cycles became official in 1995. Mitchell says, "How a person judges success depends on what he has at any given time. So even the first year felt good, because it made me a few extra grand that I wouldn't have had otherwise." Rather than focusing on making money, he prefers to focus on the reputation of his company, believing that the money will come. "Now we're of a decent size," he says about Exile. "I finally made a smart move in life."

Some people compare Exile bikes to the early bobbed or chopped bikes of the 1950s. Mitchell acknowledges that his "flavoring," especially his earlier designs, supports that observation. "We were trying to keep a handle on that nostalgic theme."

The overriding focus at Exile is simplicity. If their latest examples continue to reflect a certain heritage, it's only because they echo the minimalist aesthetic of bikes built in a bygone era. But that doesn't mean they shun technology. Exile bikes are sprinkled with spicy six-speed transmissions, internal throttles, and other trick paraphernalia. Mitchell doesn't like to chase new technology just for the sake of it. And he tries not to let it show.

"We *minimize* the non-essential components," says Mitchell. "I like to think that if a five-year-old drew a picture of a motorcycle, he'd draw one of our bikes. They're so simplified they kind of look like a *cartoon* motorcycle." But they're not cartoonish; these are hardcore machines, bad to the proverbial bone. "We're putting solid-mounted motors in rigid frames, and our bikes vibrate as much as you might imagine. They are supposed to bring out the caveman in you."

Mitchell is all about riding, but finds that too many custom motorcycles lack dependability. They are too delicate. So he tries to create bikes that represent the best of both worlds. "It will go shoulder to shoulder with any other custom bike in the parking lot. But it has that 'own-ability' that comes with tried and tested parts. If you've made that one-off part a hundred times, you know what to expect." He is also mindful of the consequences of a crash and the difficulty of replacing handcrafted parts. "'Hey man! Remember that gas tank you made out of a waste bin and old lawnmower parts? Well, I just dragged it a hundred yards down the road. Can you make me another one?' No!"

When it comes to his artistic vision, Mitchell says, "I think that what I've done is to develop my artistic taste, if you want to call it that, in my early years. I am very narrow-minded taste wise. There is to me only one *best* looking set of exhaust pipes. So each bike I build, we don't ask the question: Should we install the best looking set of pipes or the second best? For that particular bike the *best* set of exhaust pipes is what's required.

"I wake up every morning and thank God—hangovers notwithstanding—because I love what I do for a living. I feel like the luckiest guy on the planet. Every time I walk into a room and see one of our bikes, I'm still taken aback. Even more, I'm thrilled to see someone else riding one."

Bad-ass motorcycles—the joys of owning them, the satisfaction of building them, and the thrill of watching other people getting a kick out of riding them—continues to make Russell Mitchell's life in the motorcycle industry fulfilling.

Untitled

Flat Black

Art Center College of Design
Library
1700 Lida Street
Pasadena, Calif. 91103

Silver Bike

Chapter 11

Jim Nasi

The Sugar Bear

As far as Jim Nasi is concerned, any motorcycle modified from stock is a chopper. It's just a name game, and *custom* is a suitable synonym. Nasi's bikes are about as unstock as you can get. He has little patience for pious opinions about what is or is not a "correct" chopper. He'll build motorcycles the way he wants.

"I've never considered myself an artist," Nasi says. Perhaps a consummate craftsman is a better description. He spends countless hours trying to make each motorcycle as "clean" as possible by minimizing the visual intrusions of throttle cables, brake lines, and electrical wiring. The result is that everything flows together on a Nasi motorcycle with parts fitting together as tightly as the stones in a Mayan rock wall. The parts of a real Jim Nasi chopper huddle close to the ground and take on a furtive stance, crouching on two wheels rather than leaping off the pavement.

Primarily, what sets Nasi's creations apart from run-of-the-mill bondo buckets is the tin. He uses handmade, one-off sheet-metal bodywork. Therein lies the art. Jim possesses a gift for fabricating fenders and tanks that flow seamlessly from wheel to wheel. He doesn't apply so much metal that he offends the minimalists, but the metal is always *there* and always distinctive, right down to the hallmark taillight frenched inside a big, fat fender. His hydraulically controlled, sliding-and-hiding license-plate bracket is another hallmark. He will often integrate it into the paint scheme by allowing the hollow eyes of a death head to beam blood red when the brakes are applied.

Jim's tinkering habits are deeply ingrained. As a child, when his parents bought him a new bicycle, he chopped off the extraneous parts, got rid of the reflectors, and filed down the little nubs on the frame to make it smooth and clean. It's in his genes.

"I always liked Arlen's stuff," Nasi says, referring to Arlen Ness. "He's the Godfather. He's been around the longest. He deserves the respect he gets. Arlen was a big influence on me; more so on how to treat people than just bikes."

Jim Nasi's blood type is probably 20W50. He was born in the Motor City during the heyday of choppers. His older brother, John, is the director of dealer development for Big Dog motorcycles in Wichita, Kansas. His oldest brother, Jeff, is a car nut who works for *Hot Rod* magazine.

In the 1980s, Jim Nasi began to take an interest in big-twin motorcycles. After high school, Jim studied engineering at New Mexico State University in Las Cruces. "I couldn't get into it," he complains. "I didn't like what I was doing at all." After quitting college, he moved to Phoenix . There, he really got the bite for bikes. He bought a couple of 1981 Shovelheads, customized them, and rode them. He learned a lot from those two Harleys. Jim still owns one of the Shovelheads, which he has restored and is keeping for his son.

Nasi started out building and servicing custom bikes at Paragon, which eventually became Titan Motorcycle Company. Jim was employee number one at Titan. He began supervising two other employees, and soon became the production manager of a company with a workforce of 70 people reporting to him. "Once I became production manager," he says, "it wasn't about motorcycles anymore. So I left."

Nasi opened his first shop and showroom in the upscale Phoenix suburb of Scottsdale. His location, right next door to a Ferrari dealership, brought in the high-dollar crowd and helped him get a foothold in the market for exotic motorcycles.

Jim acknowledges that the chopper style, now riding the crest of fashion, has been around for 40 years, notwithstanding a bit of hibernation here in America. But he believes its current popularity will stick around for quite a long time. He thinks the current rise in popularity is due, in part, to an

American backlash against modernistic, European-influenced designs in general; not just motorcycles. "You can even see it in cars," says Nasi. "Look at the retro automobile designs coming out of Detroit. It's a return to 'old school' style.

"The years fly by so fast now," says Jim. "I'm doing my hobby for a living. I don't have much time for anything else." Jim gets some riding in from time to time. He'll put anywhere from 200 to 500 miles on a customer's new bike to break it in and make sure everything is working correctly. He hasn't built a bike for himself in quite a while, but he's planning one right now. "Picture a 1950 Merc on two wheels," he says. "It's going to have air suspension, front and rear. The frame actually sits on the ground with no kickstand. It'll have a [typically Nasi-style] big rear fender. It'll shoot flames out the pipes. The works!"

The last time Jim was pulled over by a motorcycle cop, he was riding his beloved Camel bike. At the time, it had no license-plate bracket, let alone the plate itself, no turn signals, and the dual downdraft stacks were poking wickedly out one side. Not very legal! They stopped on the shoulder of a highway adjacent to a storm drain. The cop had an attitude and was sharing it with Jim. While Officer Friendly was trying to read the VIN number on Jim's frame, the ticket book he had left on the seat of his Police Special was blown by a gust of wind into the gutter. Every ticket he had written that day was lost except Jim's, which was in the cop's hand: a $534 fine! Quite a number of speeding scofflaws owe Jim Nasi big-time.

Nasi wants to keep his production numbers low. He explains, "I don't want to pump out a production bike. But to survive, you start making parts. All these years I've been putting other peoples' parts on bikes, having to massage them and make them work. I always swore that when I make my own parts, they're gonna be perfect. You can take them out of the box and you can put them on. I'm real anal about that stuff. So much so that's it's taken me a long time to get a lot of stuff done. But rest assured that when the parts go on, they're gonna fit just right." He's adamant about that goal.

In the end, it's only quality that counts. Jim is indeed a big bear of a man, but he doesn't make his presence overwhelming. In fact, he's a quiet guy. He believes that people buy his choppers and parts from him because they're cool, not because he's cool. But Jim is definitely cool.

Untitled

Untitled

Untitled

Chapter 12

Arlen Ness

The Godfather

PEOPLE IN THE KNOW CALL ARLEN NESS THE "GODFATHER," not because he makes offers you can't refuse, but as a sign of respect for his accomplishments throughout a long and storied career. At 64, he is the patriarch of the custom motorcycle industry.

Back when choppers were still the homespun products of local craftsmen equipped with torches, hacksaws, drill presses, and rattle cans of flat black paint, Arlen Ness was going for baroque. He gold-plated parts, adorned the aluminum fascia of drivetrain components with ornate engravings, and applied wild splashes of color to the sheet metal. Plush, velour upholstery adorned his seats. If Arlen thought he could squeeze more than one motor into a frame, he would. It was nearly routine—at least for Arlen Ness—to cram two supercharged Ironhead Sportster engines into a single frame where they would cuddle up to produce ungodly heaps of horsepower.

These eccentric-looking machines defined early 1970s chopper style. Ness was one of the first chopper builders to embrace the extravagant style of the hippie counterculture that blossomed in the San Francisco Bay Area, a place Ness calls home. Ness combined "flower power" with horsepower to create motorcycles that defined an era.

"In 1965, ape-hanger handlebars combined with a peanut tank and a 21-inch front wheel: that's what choppers were *then*," recounts Ness. Extended fork tubes hadn't hit the street scene yet. Ness says that earlier examples of modified bikes, called "bobbers" and "diggers," probably evolved from flat-track Harley race bikes. Ness recalls that Denver Mullins of Denver's Choppers in Riverside, California, started making long bikes in the late 1960s. Riders called them choppers.

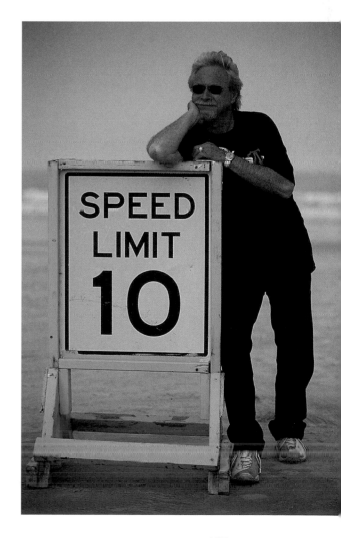

Mullins might have been popularizing the chopper in southern California, but back on Arlen's home turf, the digger was still the style *du jour*. Ness' ideas of what a custom motorcycle should be evolved into something that incorporated elements of both southern and northern California style. His idea of a chopper meant apes on a long, stretched-out Sportster with a short springer suspension supporting a tall front tire and a long rear fender.

Arlen's first bike was a used 1947 Harley-Davidson Knucklehead. Arlen took it apart, added a peanut gas tank, and painted it metalflake green with a vacuum cleaner converted to work with a spray rig. After winning first prize in a local bike show, he found himself with a part-time business painting hogs that brought home some much needed bacon. He became renowned in the Bay Area for painting flame jobs on tanks and fenders. He still has that Knucklehead.

It wasn't long before Arlen began working full-time as a custom motorcycle painter. He helped capitalize his new enterprise with winnings he had saved from a semi-professional bowling career.

Ness expanded his activities beyond painting motorcycles and began handcrafting custom parts and mounting them on motorcycles. It rapidly turned into a real business. "It's beyond my wildest dreams," he says. Arlen's designs created a path into the future of motorcycle customization for other builders to follow. His prowess with sheet metal became legendary. He almost single-handedly invented the theme bike. Ness was one of the first manufacturers to market a line of billet parts to consumers.

Ness builds 50 special bikes each year. He has a hand in every one-off bike that leaves his shop, whether it's fabricating a bracket or putting on the flames. When it comes

to major assembly, such as installing a motor, he has it down to a science. He just tells his crew what he wants, and it's done. "I've always been more of a cosmetics guy than a motor builder," he confesses.

Arlen Ness has kept every bike he built for himself since 1967. Actually, some he had to buy back from customers. He has almost 60 of them in his collection today.

Arlen believes there's no reason an excellent custom motorcycle or chopper can't be built from catalog parts by a talented builder. "Aftermarket parts are so good nowadays. It's come so far in the last 10 years, you don't have to get out the grinder and the file anymore," he says. However, when pressed, Ness admits that one criterion for making a bike rise above the rest is the contribution of a creative artist's hand to the fabrication of parts that are truly unique. All other things being equal, only then does a motorcycle rise to the level of art.

Arlen thinks it's a great thing that choppers have become popular again. "Corporate executives buy choppers now. People get plenty of attention riding choppers. They just like them. They're fun!" Ness has seen motorcycle fashions come and go, but says, "Choppers are here to stay, at least for another 10 or 15 years. Riding choppers has become more of a hobby than a lifestyle." When asked if outlaw bikers still ride, Ness replies, "Oh sure. That's their life. That's what they choose to do."

Arlen makes as much time to ride as possible, more now than before. He rides to Sturgis every year. He meets several times each year with his buddies who have formed a club consisting of custom bike owners and a few other builders like Dave Perewitz and Donnie Smith. They call themselves the Hamsters.

The Hamsters started out as an inside joke amongst riding buddies who would hook up at the major bike rallies such as in Sturgis every summer. There are now about 200 members around the world who wear the yellow T-shirt emblazoned with the scary, little rodent. In 2002, Arlen and his son, Cory, who now runs the administrative side of the business and has a hand in custom design, led 100 Hamsters from the San Francisco Bay Area to Sturgis with a television crew in tow to document the run. The Hamsters always manage to have fun en route to any destination. There's no rush to get anywhere. Parties are planned along the way. "It's pretty neat to see that many custom bikes going cross-country," says Arlen.

Arlen Ness feels he is a very fortunate man to have made a successful business doing what he loves and have kept his family close by. These days Arlen just rides, builds bikes, and plays with his four grandkids. He's happy to have been at the right place at the right time and to have persevered.

Untitled

Hippie Sporty

Long Bike

Flame Job

Art Center College of Design
Library
1700 Lida Street
Pasadena, Calif. 91103

Yellow Bird

Chapter 13

Dave Perewitz

The Yankee Chopper

In the suburban hamlet of Bridgewater, Massachusetts, an ebullient and friendly fellow named Dave Perewitz builds, in his own words, "long stretched-out, slammed-on-the-ground *stuff*." He's referring to building choppers, a genre that he defines in explicit terms. "By every sense of the word, it means a bike that is long. The frame is extended upward, so it has a high neck and a long front end. They've got a lot of rake and a lot of stretch upward. The tank is usually mounted very high on the frame. That's basically the look of a chopper."

The shape of his gas tanks and the intricate, beautiful paint he lays on his creations define Perewitz's signature style. But every now and then, he builds a bike not at all like a typical Perewitz custom, but not like anyone else's either. Dave admits, "Not every bike has 'The Look'; even that we build." A bike with The Look, he says, "has got all the lines just right. And, yes, it's all a fashion statement. No doubt about it. It's keeping up with the trends and moving on to new trends.

"There is almost nothing we can't handle," says Perewitz. "Back in the old days it wasn't like today. No matter what kinds of problems we encounter we can fix them. When you've been doing this stuff for 30 years, it comes pretty natural. I don't know how the people who've been doing this for only a few years can avoid letting snags turn into fiascos."

Perewitz opened his first shop, Cycle Fabrications, in 1975 and, in the ensuing decades, has learned just about everything concerning custom motorcycle building. "There's so much involved in making stuff work," he says, "because it's not just one thing; it's a whole train of events. There are so many things that have to fit together. There're so many parts that aren't interchangeable. You can change one thing, but when you change

163

five things, they're a mismatch and they don't fit. It unravels the thread. Because I've been in the industry so long and I know everybody, I know who's got the good stuff and who doesn't. Even at that you run into problems. If we didn't have a full machine shop here, we'd be screwed."

When asked if he considers himself an artist, Perewitz responds, "Yeah, I guess I do, even though I can't draw worth a shit." He lays out all the flames and sprays them. "I've been a painter most of my life. For 15 or 20 years, I did *all* the paint work. I design the lines of the bikes. But when we build bikes, I rarely draw sketches because I can picture in my mind just what something's going to look like. As we're building it, I can see it before it's done."

Dave Perewitz does not believe that anyone can build a piece of art by purchasing parts from a catalog. He sees no artistry in bikes that are bolted together from cookie-cutter parts that were put in a box by someone in the marketing department—or even some other builder for that matter. To him it would be like paining by numbers. "It has to have that special touch," says Perewitz. "If you're buying stuff out of a catalog, you're not a good enough artist to make it look that way."

Perewitz says, "We do two things here for the most part. We build 'ground-up' bikes and we do what we call a 'heavy facelift.'" The latter starts out with a new or slightly used stock bike that gets torn down to parts. But Perewitz leaves the motors in the frame. The frame is raked, the tank is stretched, and it will get new wheels and fenders. They'll add new brakes and some chrome here and there. Since most of the "facelift" jobs start with Harley-Davidson Twin-cam models, he'll also install, in-house, a 95-inch hop-up kit for more power.

Generally speaking, most of Dave's customers don't have pre-conceived ideas of what they want their new bikes to look like, other than that they should exhibit the Perewitz style. Being the maestro gives Perewitz complete creative control. He still will always elicit some kind of a direction by listening to what a particular customer *doesn't* want. "One of the biggest hindrances, believe it or not," Dave says, "has been the Internet. You've got these guys that sit at home in front of the computer looking at hundreds of parts, and they start making lists. Most of the time, I just nix it all, or most of it

"We have a firm rule around here," says Dave: "We don't become attached to motorcycles. We build 'em, we sell 'em. It's a business." For example, Perewitz recounts the story of a bike he designed in the late 1980s. "I built a rubber-mount, five-inch-stretch Ness frame with a swingarm. We built the motor with dual carburetors. I turned one head around backwards, so I had two front heads; and I had one carburetor coming out one side and one carburetor coming out the other." It was a trend-setting design; cutting edge for its time. Recently, its owner approached Dave to see if he was interested in buying it back. He considered the offer carefully but declined, because he was afraid he couldn't keep himself from tearing it down and redoing it, despite the fact that if he bought it, he should preserve it as is. You see, it was cutting edge *then*, but not now. He's like an author who can't keep from rewriting what he's already done.

Around the Perewitz shop a motto prevails: *Choppers are for kids*. Dave doesn't see too many older guys riding choppers, except perhaps for throwbacks who never gave up the greasy sleds they rode back in the day. He sees a different and younger clientele drawn to choppers today. The older riders who have been responsible for the surge of growth in the motorcycle market tend to ride bikes with more creature comforts, more in tune with middle-aged butts and backs. But younger chopper riders may be expanding the market further instead of usurping a part of it. Choppers may be the right catalyst to add vibrant, young enthusiasts to the crowd of older riders.

What choppers may *look* like in the future is anybody's guess. "Choppers are kind of like flames," says Dave. "They become very popular at times and then less popular; but they're always going to be there."

Untitled

Untitled

Chapter 14

Bob Phillip

Meet Mr. Wizard

On a quiet cul-de-sac in south Florida near Boca Raton lives an artist full of surprises. His graceful vases are the delight of interior decorators and art galleries, but he makes motorcycles that cause concussive damage to the internal organs of anyone in the vicinity. These astonishing machines spring from the mind of a man who's been known as the Wizard since he was a kid.

Bob Phillip learned early in life that technology is merely subject to the disposition of his imagination. When hammers, hacksaws, grinders, and welders aren't enough, he'll resort to sorcery to do the trick. He once sacrificed the still-beating heart of a brand new Ducati sportbike to the gods of motorcycle customization. Although whether or not one might call the resulting machine a chopper is debatable.

"I would probably call a chopper—obviously with the word *chop*—something that's been cut up, sliced, diced, sectioned, beaten, painted," Bob says in his deep, gravelly voice. "An accumulation of miscellaneous parts, whether it be from an old car or a motorcycle. Obviously a long front end or some type of sinister rake on it; that's probably what I'd call a chopper." Phillip believes that a chopper is less about what you're looking at and better defined by how it makes you feel. "It's a change-in-your-personality kind of thing, getting on a chopper," he says.

Phillip seldom purchases parts. "Parts are a problem for me. Parts that I buy don't fit or the chrome's no good. That's why I choose to build as many pieces as I can. It's *my* name on a customer's bike if it's broken down by the side of the road, whether it's my fault or not. So I'd rather, if it's broken down, it *is* my fault, not somebody else's."

Phillip's bikes are built to be ridden hard. "I have built a few that are lookers," he says, "but while I look at a motorcycle as being a piece of art, a Picasso hanging up on a wall by a nail, why not be able to ride this painting?"

Phillip's father, Bob Sr., was manager of assembly at Piper Aircraft in Vero Beach, Florida. Bob Jr., practically grew up inside the plant and learned his mechanical skills from people who worked for his father.

"My parents always kept an apron around me," Bob says. "I wasn't allowed to do this, and I wasn't allowed to do that." To keep their curious child out of mischief, they installed a workshop on the patio in back of their house. Bob helped enclose the structure so he could work on his various projects rain or shine. "I didn't go to the movies; I didn't go to football games like the other kids." Instead, he learned how to weld.

Although his parents tried to protect Bob Jr., from pursuits they perceived as dangerous, by the time the Wizard was 14, he had secretly purchased his first motorcycle, a Honda 70 that he kept at a friend's house and rode surreptitiously. "They were shocked when they found out," he says of his parents. By the time he was 16, Bob bought his first Harley. Before that, he always had the "baddest" bicycles. He cut them up and welded them back together again. They were his first choppers.

It's a slippery slope from bicycle customization to motorcycle customization, and eventually Phillip succumbed. While operating an independent Mercedes-Benz garage in New England, he built custom motorcycles on the side for fun. After he won every custom bike show in New England, he thought he would stack up his bikes against the West Coast competition, so he packed off to California and won another 15 trophies right off the bat at the Del Mar Antique Motorcycle Show. "Been there, done that, won that," says the

Wizard. Photo shoots for the enthusiast magazines ensued and brought him some national exposure.

By this time, Phillips decided to move back to Florida. The folks at *Easyrider* magazine explained that this was Eddie Trotta territory and suggested that Bob see Eddie about a job. He started working for Eddie the very day they met. "I learned a shit load from him," says Bob. "He is an institution in this business. I can only thank him. I wouldn't be as strong as I am now if it wasn't for Eddie Trotta."

Bob calls himself a glorified welder. "The TIG torch is my paintbrush," he says. "I can make things happen with that and a hammer." He has always had a gift to see how metal bends. He sees the grain in it. "One wrong smash with the hammer and you stretch the metal too far, and it will never go back to shape," he warns.

The work that the Wizard does is so meticulous that it took 37 hours to create a single carburetor velocity stack from a chunk of billet aluminum. There are no CNC machines here. This is all handmade, or as Bob calls it, "hand-cobbled" work. Of course there are only a few people who can afford to pay for bikes with that much time and effort invested in their manufacture. Only a few are made each year with that degree of detail.

"Everybody who wants a chopper has a bad side. When somebody comes to me wanting a motorcycle built, he wants to be like me. Not that I'm cool, but people think I'm cool because I ride cool stuff. And he wants to get out of his shell. He wants to be another person for the weekend. So he comes out of the office on Friday with a little five-o'clock shadow. By Saturday he's a little mean-looking. Tattoo parlor next. Monday it's back in the Porsche, back in the Bentley; back to the office."

Phillip says he develops a different relationship with his customers than he would if he did anything besides building motorcycles for a living. He tells how a corporate mucky-muck might get a telephone call at the office: "I need to speak to Mr. Smith. This is his wife." His secretary says he's in a board meeting and cannot be disturbed. Or it can be: "I need to speak to Mr. Smith about his *car*." Same deal; he can't come to the phone. But if it's Bob Phillip calling to speak to Mr. Smith about his motorcycle: "Hold on please, Mr. Phillip. He'll be right with you." The guy comes on the line, interrupting his board meeting, *sotto voce*. "Bob, I can't talk right now. What's up? Do whatever you need to do. I want to ride this weekend. I'll talk to you Saturday." That's when Bob gets ready for his next adventure.

Speed Merchant

Untitled

Chapter 15

Pontarelli

Harold Pontarelli's Unassuming Sophistication

IF YOU CAN LOOK PAST HIS CLASSIC BIKER APPEARANCE—unruly red hair, long scraggly beard, colorful tattoos—you will see that Harold Pontarelli is a nice guy. Unfortunately though, unconventional looks can make opinionated people jump to preposterous conclusions. For instance, Pontarelli dodged his only scrape with the law because he had broken both of his arms and legs after plunging into the windshield of a car.

A vehicle swerved into his lane of traffic and hit him head on at 60 miles per hour. The unscathed driver of the offending vehicle offered him a napkin to keep the blood off her upholstery. To add insult to an appallingly painful injury, the police who arrived on the scene threatened Harold with arrest. Since he was clearly of the "outlaw-biker" persuasion, the cops just assumed he was at fault. Perhaps they figured he was breaking and entering the hard way! In spite of the fact that he was already immobilized and his motorcycle had become a hood ornament, handcuffs were fended off only by adamant paramedics who refused to surrender custody of their patient.

Like most of his colleagues who breathe the rarefied air of custom bike builders (or maybe it's just the paint fumes), Harold Pontarelli is an eccentric fellow. Still, one gets the idea that he probably works because he wants to and not because he has to, though he is vague on the subject.

Harold was born in 1960 in Santa Monica, California, to parents who were, he says rather ambiguously, "in the building trades." When asked to elaborate, he only says they were involved in the high-rise construction business. "Remember," he says, "my name is *Pontarelli*."

Pontarelli will describe any number of different ways to build a chopper without trying to pin down an exact definition. The fact that everybody has a different idea of what a chopper should be allows creativity to flourish. As far as the Pontarelli school of chopper design is concerned, a chopper only has to be gorgeous.

He doesn't subscribe to the criterion that choppers are required to have extended forks. Not even in the old days of bobbing fenders and chopping frames was it considered necessary for a bike to have an elongated front end, he says. Pontarelli asserts that many 1970s-era choppers in the San Francisco Bay Area actually had short front forks. His father owned a long bike with forks 20 inches over. "Maybe it was 30!" he says upon reflection. At any rate, it was grotesque, even by the freewheeling standards of the time. As a kid, he thought it looked "neat."

The kinds of choppers that his father and his father's friends owned were so whacked out they weren't practical to ride except in straight lines with a kidney belt. Ultimately, they went the way of the dinosaurs. His father's chopper is long gone, but *the* very chopper that first captured his attention as a teenager growing up in east of the Bay now lies under a layer of dust in the back of his shop. By today's standards, it's a strange-looking machine. Every part that would be polished or chromed today was plated with real gold. Built in 1974 by a very young Ron Simms, it has a supercharged, Ironhead Sportster motor, springer suspension, plush seat, and a lot of ornate engravings and curlicues in the paint scheme. A twist of luck and fate brought it back into Harold's life. Six months before his son was born, a friend inquired if he was interested in seeing a rather unusual

Sportster. It was the same bike he grew up admiring as a kid. His friend couldn't resist presenting this relic to Harold as a gift so he could restore it for his son to ride one day.

Harold believes that if he refuses to give up searching, he'll find more dinosaurs lurking in lost garages. He will buy and restore them whenever they turn up, but most of them have been cannibalized of their girders, springers, king-and-queen seats, and high-rise smoke stacks for spare parts.

Pontarelli's biggest pet peeve is a customer who doesn't respect the high degree of devotion and the grueling work that goes into creating a custom motorcycle. He is offended by those who would treat works of art as mere status symbols. One ignoramus took delivery of a brand-new custom sled adorned with Pontarelli parts and paint, and peeled rubber right out of the parking lot. There's nothing wrong with showing off, but this just wasn't the right application for the kind of motorcycle Harold had built for this guy. He careened across the asphalt, launched off the curb, and landed hard, taking out the rear fender and saddle bags. It was the end of that relationship. "Can you fix it?" asked the rider" "No, I'm done," replied the maestro. "I'm done with *you*, dude."

While Pontarelli has a penchant for heaps of horsepower and stump-pulling torque, he holds off just a bit with choppers. "I love building really fast motors, but I try not to build a real fast motor in a chopper because the bike doesn't handle as well. The faster you go, the more you're going to put yourself in a bind. I like building very exotic motors with blowers and turbos, but they don't really fit the lines of a chopper."

Fashion trends in motorcycles come and go. When Harold was only 14 years old, he built an 8-inch-over Panhead Springer. He had already decided that his father's long bike was passé, so this was his first attempt to take some old and new ideas and make something altogether his own.

By the late 1980s when Pontarelli first began to take professional commissions, the market still primarily called for retro-style bikes with fat front tires and lots of sheet metal. Building award-winning bikes like that kept him busy, but he remained aware of the choppers that colleagues like Pat Kennedy and Eddie Trotta continued to crank out. Pontarelli believes Trotta instigated the resurgence of the long front end. Both Kennedy and Trotta have remained true to the chopper ethos throughout the years, never abandoning their roots. Harold admires their dedication and style. Eventually he decided to try his own hand at building another chopped sled, and hasn't stopped building choppers since. His bikes are now among the hottest in the world.

Pontarelli only builds one-of-a-kind bikes that are practical to ride. He won't copy anything he's done in the past, so you can trust that the bike he builds for you will be the only one on the planet. He paints them himself, and don't ever ask Harold Pontarelli to paint a chopper black! Black choppers don't fit into Pontarelli's aesthetic visions, which is what customers are ultimately paying him for. He'll take their cash and give them an amazing bike, but if they ruin it, that's their tough luck.

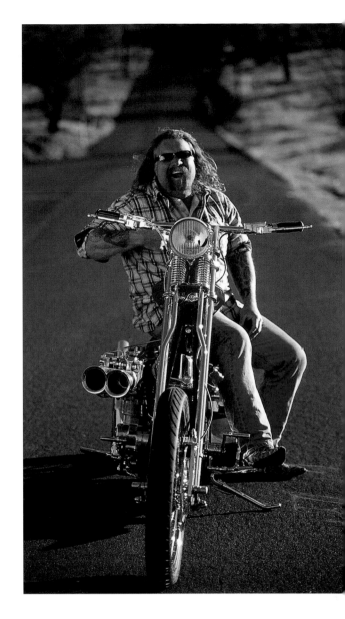

ART CENTER COLLEGE OF DESIGN LIBRARY

Untitled

Toxic Green

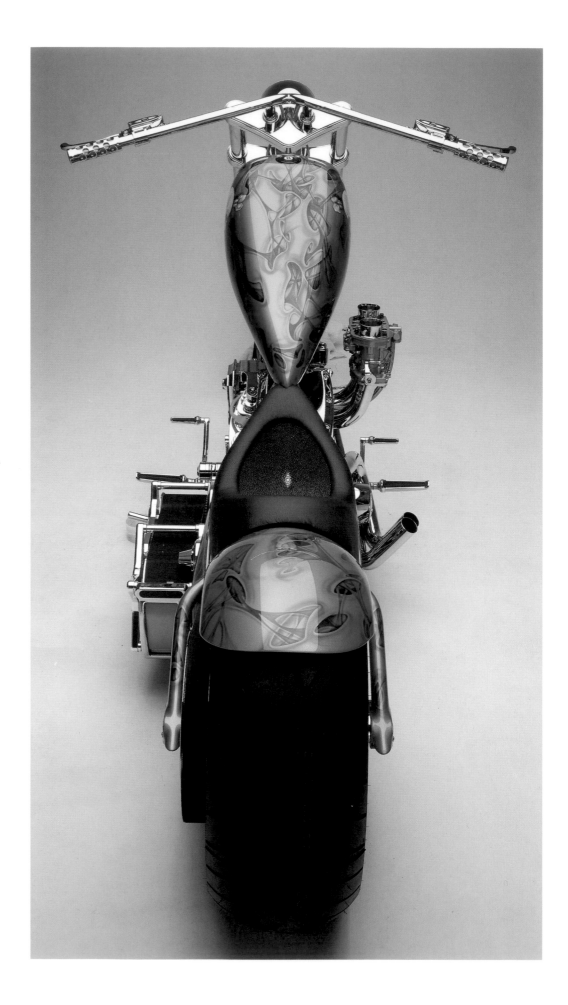

Untitled

Chapter 16

Ron Simms

The Thug

AFTER 30-PLUS YEARS OF BUILDING CUSTOM BIKES, Ron Simms presides over a small empire. He says he never lies about anything or to anyone except cops. His voice is as rough as his talk is tough and there are always some Hell's Angels around his shop in Hayward, California. He has trademarked the name "Thug" for the big-inch motors in his bigger-than-life bikes. With the exception of his paint jobs, he sees things in black and white and has little patience for nuance.

Simms, who grew up near the San Francisco Bay, says, "Bikes have been a way of life in the Bay Area. For whatever reasons, they're not unusual around here."

The Bay Area motorcycle scene has fascinated Simms since before he can remember. At the age of 6 or 7, Ron became fascinated with the complexities of a Knucklehead bagger. A decrepit Indian Chief ended up on his family's back porch when he was 12 and Ron would have given anything to ride that motorcycle. He sat on it and pretended to ride it for hours at a time, shifting and imitating motor noises. At one point in the mid-1960s, not too long before the motorcycle bug *really* bit him, a friend drove Ron out to Angel's Camp, a ghost town in Calaveras County. The two teenage boys went to ogle the good-looking girls hanging out with older guys riding diggers. They looked gnarly—the guys *and* the bikes—and were rather intimidating to high school kids. Ron and his buddy kept quiet; they just walked around and took in the scene. They found themselves spending more time looking at the bikes than they did looking at the girls. The bikers turned out to be friendly and spoke to the boys, explaining how they had customized their motorcycles. That experience made a lasting impression on Ron.

Simms has a natural mechanical aptitude—he can fix anything with some hand tools, a grinding wheel, and a drill press—and he became the go-to guy for local bikers. If he needed to make a spacer, he started with a piece of pipe, cut it with a hacksaw, and bored it out with a drill. That's how it was done in the day.

He didn't spend all of his time in the garage, though. Ron wanted to ride, too. At some point he laid hands on a basket case for himself. He got it running and completely restored it, painting it pearl white with candy red flames, which was a real novelty back then. Someone offered to buy it and made him an offer too good to pass up: twice the price of a brand new Harley-Davidson! They cost only about $1,800 at the time. Motivated by this financial success, he searched for more basket cases, and he soon had a garage full of bikes to sell.

Simms invested his new-found wealth into a house with a large garage where he could work on more than one motorcycle at a time. He turned stock baggers and Sportys into choppers with short front ends and long frames. Similar to Arlen Ness during the same period, he began to make very ornate bikes, sometimes with gold plating instead of chrome, a lot of engraving, plush seats, sissy bars, and highly-modified Harley-Davidson motors. That was the epitome of the East Bay style. By 1972, Ron was doing well enough to buy a small building that had once accommodated a Harley-Davidson dealership.

If you ask Ron Simms what a chopper is, he'll tell you that the first custom motorcycle was essentially a chopper, and that's how it all started. "For me it means more of an old school design than a current design." That's his personal taste. He makes a further distinction by saying that the newer designs are "retro choppers, not choppers." Ron says, "The chopper style has really never gone out. With some guys it's been a mainstay. Some guy that was building choppers thirty years ago is probably doing the same thing now. But maybe it's long and low, or fat. Whatever!"

It's good for Simms that "old school" is hot right now. He's building bikes once again with old-fashioned jockey shifts because that's what clients want; although he might give it a hydraulic clutch, a fat rear tire, and a 120-inch motor. He has nothing against technology.

What's changed about choppers is not so much the bikes, but how they are perceived. Simms remembers, "Ten years ago, what a lot of these younger guys don't understand, is we physically couldn't ride our bikes in certain parts of L.A., especially around Hollywood and Beverly Hills. If we got close, they'd pull us over. Now we do shows on Rodeo Drive."

There are some builders with whom Simms has cultivated friendships, but there's always a little competitive thing going on. "And for anybody to say that there wasn't, they'd flat out be lying," declares Simms. "There's friends of mine that are in the business; we kind of compete, like somebody'll call up—maybe like Eddie Trotta—and he'll call up and he goes, 'Hey man, I just did this and this …' And I have to come back and say, 'Well, I did that eight years ago.' So there's always a bit of one-upmanship."

Simms is definitely a competitor. He wants his bikes to be a little faster than anybody else's. "Maybe a little flashier, too," he adds.

A theme perpetuated by Simms—it's stamped onto many of his retail parts—is the symbol of the double-S lightning bolts. He's quick to point out that it does not have anything to do with Nazi SS storm troopers. Lightning bolts have long been associated in Hawaii with surfing culture, and that's what it represents on a Simms chopper.

Simms wants people to pay attention to his bikes. His clients pay him large sums of money because they want other people to look at them! The whole experience of riding a Simms chopper is characterized by a profane pummeling of ordinary human sensibilities. He claims that anyone can distinguish a Simms bike by the sound of the exhaust blasted through tuned pipes by his Thug motor, which Simms has manufactured to his specifications.

Simms says, "I'm always thinking in a progressive state." The plans for his next build are present in his mind before the rubber hits the road for his current project. "If I ever built the perfect bike, I'd keep it forever and I'd stop building bikes," Simms says, "but I'll never build a perfect bike. This is what I'll be doing forever."

Gold Sporty

Shark

Untitled

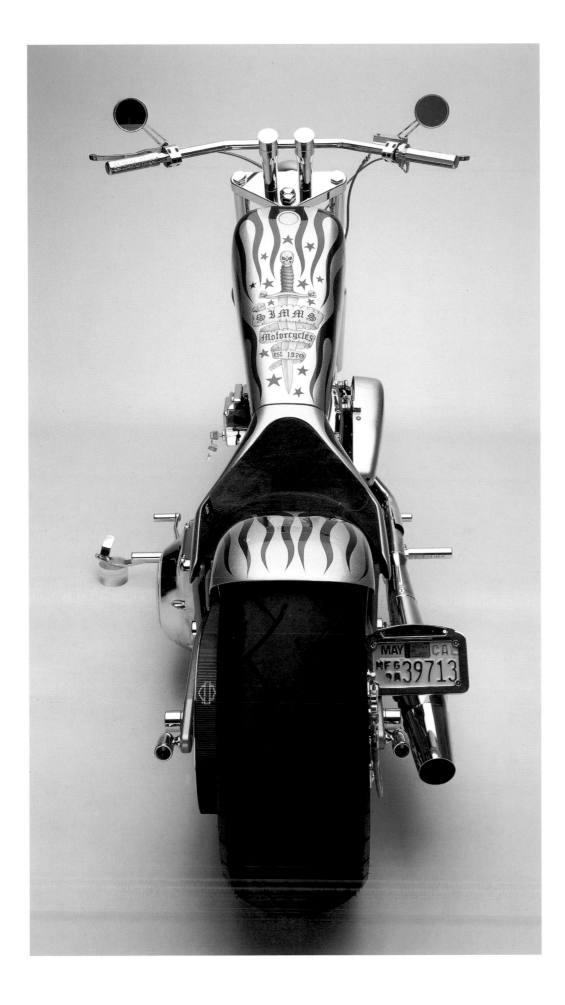

Liberace

Fuck Luck

Chapter 17

Donnie Smith

All-American Farm Boy

"BIKING IS ONE OF THE LAST THINGS YOU CAN DO TO GIVE YOURSELF A LITTLE FLAVOR of the outlaw side of things," Donnie Smith says. "We're really cowboys on wheels. It's all about being free. Even with a group, it's hard to communicate while you're doing 60-70 miles per hour. You tend to keep to yourself."

Born in the spring of 1942 in Donnelly, a town of 300 souls in western Minnesota, Smith was raised on his parents' dairy farm. By the time Donnie graduated from high school, he knew he wanted to race dragsters, not drive tractors; so he came to the big city of St. Paul, Minnesota.

Donnie's first experiences with motorcycles left him gun shy. When he was 16 years old, he hopped on a friend's Panhead Harley and rode it right up onto a curb. It was a bit more of a handful than he expected. Then, in 1962, his Uncle Elwood offered Smith a ride on a hopped-up Sportster; "a real cammy bike," recalls Smith. Donnie rode it down to the corner on the wet, cobblestone street, made a U-turn, then rode back up the street and made another U-turn. That didn't go too badly, so Donnie went down the street once again to make another U-turn, but Donnie said, "The bike kinda sneezed and I grabbed a handful of throttle." It took off with Donnie hanging on for dear life, jumped the curb, and hit a retaining wall with a wire fence that caught the throttle. Donnie was dragged down the sidewalk a few painful yards. He suffered some nasty raspberries down his leg and swore off bikes.

One winter day a couple of years later a friend offered Donnie a ride on his Triumph. "You can't get hurt," said his friend. "If you fall down, you've got four inches of snow to protect you."

ART CENTER COLLEGE OF DESIGN LIBRARY

The Triumph felt good. "Hell," Donnie thought, "This isn't so bad." Pretty soon he was zipping up and down the roadway. Nothing happened! Shortly after that, Donnie found a year-old Triumph for sale and bought it on January 31, 1964. From then on, any day that was above 32 degrees Fahrenheit, he and his friends would ride. By the summer of that first year, he had logged 10,000 miles on his own Triumph. "We rode them things," he remembers fondly. "We lived on them."

When Smith got out of the Army in 1970, *Easy Rider* had just hit the silver screen. It was the fuse that ignited the chopper bomb. Before then, choppers had been around, but were confined to the culture of the one-percenters. Now they were introduced to mainstream society.

After the army, Donnie opened an auto parts shop with his brother and a friend. One day, his uncle Elwood came by with a motorcycle frame he wanted raked. Donnie chopped the frame and welded it back together on a Sunday afternoon. The stylishly stretched-out motorcycle impressed other riders in the vicinity. Soon the shop manufactured motorcycle frames full time, followed shortly by the manufacture of entire custom motorcycles.

They printed their first business cards in 1971. The business exploded and grew to 15 employees within a few years.

Donnie became a regular at Sturgis and other rallies. He got to know other builders and struck up a close friendship with Arlen Ness and Dave Perewitz. Like his fellow Hamsters, Smith enjoys riding choppers even more than building them. He recently rode a chopper all the way from Florida to Texas alongside Dave Perewitz and Billy Lane, which was captured on Discovery channel's "The Great Biker Build-Off."

By the time a typical Harley owner has finished bolting on every conceivable part he can find and he's thinking that his bike looks too much like every other one in the parking lot, "He becomes *mine!*" whispers Smith feigning a greedy grin. "We'll cut the frame, do a little rake on it, stretch the tank, do something with the fenders, and put a wild paint job on it." The company receives 8 to 12 commissions each year from customers.

Regarding individual style, Donnie says, "Everybody [meaning only the best of his colleagues] has their own little thing that they do. People tell me that my bikes 'always just sit right.'" That's a comment he hears regularly from magazine editors, too. Like any great builder, lines are important to Smith, but achieving the correct proportions, or scale, in addition to that is vital. No component is too big or small, or too long or wide on a Donnie Smith motorcycle. Smith tries to avoid the possibility of a sudden interruption, "an x," as he puts it, that might divert your eyes from any fluid arc of material structure. "There's a certain line [to my bikes] that makes me who I am."

"Up to a point," Smith says, carefully choosing his words, "I guess I consider myself an artist." He doesn't make a large distinction between style and art, or a devotion to craftsmanship. Donnie is candid about his lack of sophistication when it comes to art: "I know absolutely nothing about Picasso. I don't get that." But he knows choppers. He believes that if a bike is rough around the edges, it should not command a top price.

"It's all part of what we do," Donnie says. "Anybody might look at any of my bikes and say it's a piece of glass, it's a trailer bike, you can't use them or ride them. Well, we *do* use them and ride them. We ride them all the time. Everybody's got their opinion. And so I think in this industry everybody respects what everybody does."

When asked about some of the young Turks whose attitude implies that they reinvented the chopper, Donny says, "Excuse me? Choppers were around when some of these guys were still in diapers." Donnie doesn't claim to be one of the originators himself, but he certainly has contributed to its stylistic evolution and the body of art. "These guys are helping it along, too," he says, "but there ain't nothing new. They're just warming up another pan of soup."

Smith feels most comfortable with his friends in the motorcycle business. "It's an interesting sport. I'm proud to be part of it." He enjoys his jaunts to familiar haunts around the country with the Hamsters. Donnie has only one idiosyncrasy about riding motorcycles: He won't wear black. "What bikers wear changes their attitude," he gripes. He thinks that donning black leathers, as so many riders do, gives them an ornery demeanor. He has too much fun to be ornery.

Although he may be just a little grayer, Donnie Smith is as forthright, sincere, freedom-loving, fun-loving, and ambitious as any red-blooded American farm boy of 18.

Redneck Rocket

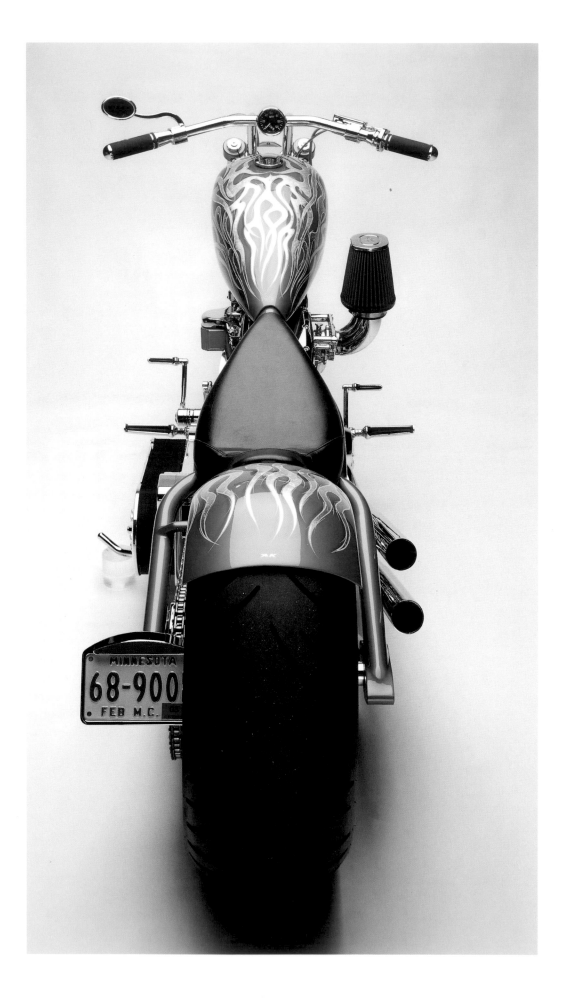

Untitled

Untitled

Untitled

Untitled

Chapter 18

The Teutuls

Everything is Relative

TALK ABOUT FOLLOWING IN YOUR FATHER'S FOOTSTEPS! Paul Teutul Jr. and his father, Paul Sr., work together, and often at odds with each other, six days a week in the crowded shop they call Orange County Choppers. Located in Orange County, New York, the tiny town of Rock Tavern is home to OCC and the extended Teutul family. What began as a father-and-son bike project in the basement of Paul Sr.'s house quickly led to a booming enterprise, thanks to the notoriety their debut effort received at Biketoberfest in Daytona Beach, Florida, in 1999. Orders for custom choppers poured in from dozens of eager riders and led to the founding of OCC that same year.

Born in Yonkers, New York, in 1949, Paul Teutul Sr. survived some "bad times," his vague description of his battle with substance abuse before he started manufacturing wrought iron fixtures for homeowners. Still in his twenties, he moved from Brooklyn to Orange County and started a family. Paul Jr., the eldest of four children, was born in 1974.

When he lived in Brooklyn in the early 1970s, Paul Sr., owned a Triumph. Paul watched his buddies tear down their chopped Harleys, stretch the frames, build tanks and fenders from sheet metal, hop up their motors, and then put everything back together again, and he was inspired.

Paul still owns a 1974 Harley that he bought new. Paul Jr. "Pauly" grew up watching his father perform mechanical magic on that Shovelhead. Like father, like son: the younger Teutul's interests developed in sync with the elder man's. The father recognized the son's talent, and by the time Pauly became old enough to ride, they began to work together on motorcycles. "I began working with metal and sharpening my skills at an early age," Pauly says.

What makes OCC's style particularly interesting is its focus on thematic interpretations. Theme bikes put OCC on the map—and on television. The Teutuls and OCC are now featured in a weekly television series on the Discovery Channel called *American Chopper*. The Teutuls create their signature bikes to memorialize a particular topic high on the agenda of public consciousness. They built a chopper that looks like a jet fighter plane to acknowledge the war in Afghanistan and a bike that resembles a fire engine as a tribute to the firefighters who lost their lives on September 11, 2001.

When referring to theme choppers, Pauly admits, "It's definitely more about looks than function." Nevertheless, he builds choppers that both look and perform well. "There's an aspect to choppers that dictates form over function. You try to find a happy medium." Paul and Pauly both realize that the choppers they build have to perform well when ridden. Eye-candy alone is not enough. OCC choppers "have to be able to turn as hard as you want to turn, steer comfortably, and not have things crack and fall off," Pauly explains.

Regarding the execution of a high-dollar OCC chopper, Pauly says, "It's all about the lines and pulling off the theme." According to Pauly, a bike succeeds as art only when every aspect makes a single and concise design statement. He doesn't believe that "propping" (bolting on a conglomeration of theme-related parts) a bike will make a viable chopper. Everything must be designed from scratch to work together to achieve a creative goal.

Paul says, "You can't build a bike out of a catalog and call it a custom bike."

"The truth is you *can*," disagrees his son. "You can buy the parts and build a really nice chopper. If you have a lot of money, you can part out a really nice chopper, but the bar is set really high. Who are you asking [what is a custom bike]?"

In the future, Pauly foresees technological innovation playing an increasingly large role in chopper design. "The sky's the limit—literally," he says. He looks forward to adopting space-age materials for both drivetrain components and the structural and esthetic components of future motorcycles.

In the Teutuls' neck of the woods, they've found the law to be lenient when it comes to riding a really nice chopper. "We've broken all the rules—big time," says Paul, who recalls when they were stopped once not that long ago, ostensibly for speeding, but they felt the officer might have just wanted to admire the bikes. Paul recalls, "The cop was so confused he just said, 'You know what! I think you guys better leave because we'll be here for a while if I start writing tickets.' It's the way you carry yourself. And we're not big on drinking and breaking *those* kinds of rules."

As is usually the case with a master motorcycle builder, riding time is scarce, but father and son try to get out for a putt as often as possible. They have little time for hobbies. "If I'm not working and it's nice out, I'll golf," admits the younger. When asked about his love life, the single Pauly simply replies, "Just chilling."

Paul Sr. enjoys weight lifting at the gym. "I don't golf!" exclaims the elder biker.

"Sorry, no tattoos, no piercing," Pauly points out about himself, alluding to the interesting illustrations on his father's big arms.

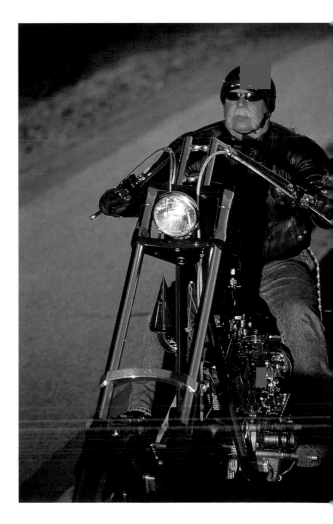

Working with his father is "a hellish nightmare of death and destruction," deadpans Pauly. More seriously, he says, "You know, it's tough; not like working for someone you don't have any ties with outside the job. It's impossible to separate the work relationship from the personal relationship." The Teutuls spend most of every day working together, dealing regularly with deadlines. Add to that the fact that, for months at a time, they have a three-person TV camera crew in their faces from 9 A.M to 5 P.M. with a one-hour break for lunch during those six days. That *is* tough.

Paul Sr. says, "There are times I'd rather stick pins in my eyes than be around Pauly. There are outside issues that don't go away just because you've crossed into a work environment." Okay, that's for the interviewer and the TV cameras. But let it be said that these guys love each other very much. Paul Sr. says, "We're a pair that will always beat a full house."

Jet Bike

Trim Spa

Black Widow

Chapter 19

Eddie Trotta

Fast Eddie

REGARDING THE NATURE OF THE CHOPPER, EDDIE TROTTA SAYS, "Some people have a different theory on it: any kind of customized motorcycle. But a chopper to me would be a stretched-out bike." Trotta believes, "It's better to look good than feel good!"

Trotta has always been true to the long bike. "I always believed in choppers. I can prove it," he says with a twinkle in his eye. "If you look at some of the bikes I built in the early nineties, before everybody was on the chopper trend, I was building stretched Softails. Not a whole bunch of stretch, but they had four to six inches in the front tubes." The prevailing style of motorcycle in the 1980s and 1990s looked "a little stubby" to Trotta who hated to see "big goons" riding down the road on what looked like "little mini bikes." Trotta says that it's better to be seen sitting in a bike than on top of it. He likes to keep the seat low and bring the tank up just high enough so the rider can sit behind it. If you sit back in a chair and hold out your arms and legs, "that's right where you want to be," Trotta says.

Trotta takes umbrage at any suggestion that long bikes originated in California. "I'm going back to the early sixties, as far as I can remember, and in Connecticut. My friend had a portable welding truck. We were in the backyard stretching frames." Eddie was 12 or 13 years old. His older brother Art had an old Knucklehead. "We stretched his frame different every year; raked the neck different every year." By 1966 it was raked out to 53 degrees with a 20 over springer front suspension. The brothers knew nothing about steering geometry in those days. "We'd just cut the neck and jump up and down on it until it was almost level, and say okay, weld it up! Nowadays, we do measure rake and trail and stuff like that."

Trotta believes the Swedes, "Tolle and those guys," who made adjustable triple trees, were the first to figure out how a simple geometric calculation improves the steering for long bikes. "If you do an enormous amount of rake without any stretch," Trotta explains, "you got a huge amount of flop, left and right, and your wheel quits steering. But if you change your rake on your trees…."

Art Trotta ran with a motorcycle club called the Slumlords back in New Haven where they grew up. Eddie enjoyed watching them come roaring by on their bikes. "They looked like a bunch of madmen. They were." The younger Trotta thought that was the coolest thing. It was his introduction to motorcycles.

The brothers and their cronies rode all summer long. When October came around and the cold set in, they'd tear their bikes down. It was unthinkable to go through a whole winter without repainting, rechroming, or stretching a motorcycle. They might even customize it with a new gas tank or fenders and have a "new" bike ready to debut for the next riding season.

"My brother's face got cut in half one night when we were riding, and when I was 17, I fell off doing a hundred miles an hour. They scraped me off the road. My mother and father wanted to have a little normal family. They ended up with two lunatics." Eddie still thinks about that high-speed spill every time he gets on a bike. "I'm not at the front of the pack any more," he says. "I like abusing a bike still, you know, hole shots, wheelies, and stuff. I'm just not into going 125 miles per hour any more. I'd rather just cruise to get there."

Eddie Trotta takes his motorcycles seriously and assumes personal responsibility for their quality. "Am I a master metal smith?" he asks. "No, I'm a hacker, but I'm a good designer."

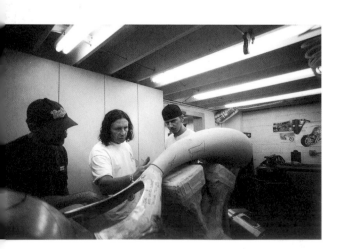

Trotta likes his bikes beefy and stretched. They exude a larger-than-life scale. He was one of the first designers to start manufacturing frames with inch-and-a-half-diameter tubing. Trotta says, "My number one priority is to make them indestructible." He says that if you go overboard with body work and paint on some show bikes, and with the huge displacements of some engines, they're not going to be as dependable after 10,000 miles as something built with more practical riding in mind. The trick is to keep things simple, yet looking good.

Trotta enjoys the work of other chopper builders. "I've always been a fan of a lot of guys: Pat Kennedy, Ron Simms, Arlen Ness. There's a guy up in New York, Mike Pugliesi. Not many people know him. He builds one bike every year."

Eddie supports independent builders if he is impressed with their technique and creativity by supplying some parts here and there or offering tips. He enjoys being a mentor. "I've always been a frustrated artist," Eddie says. "I always wished I could have drawn or painted or something. I'm a frustrated photographer. I shoot all my own catalogs and stuff."

Eddie's first professional ambition had nothing to do with motorcycles. He wanted to be a musician. He started piano lessons at the age of 5. He attended the famed Berklee School of Music in Boston. He met and heard many talented musical artists and dreamed about achieving their level of ability and success. But after years of hard work, most of them were still struggling for financial security. He questioned the wisdom of investing decades of practice to "take a bus to work and teach a class" if things didn't work out. The possibility of teaching all day and performing all night in jazz clubs didn't appeal to him.

Trotta enjoyed a successful career as a professional gambler in Florida, then another as a powerboat racer, and finally he became part owner in a motorcycle-oriented bar. While recovering from cancer, he used his down time to resume his boyhood hobby of building choppers. Trotta bought a few frames from a company called Atlas in 1991 and the chopper business really started to roll. Although he's had another bout with cancer, today Trotta's Thunder Cycles is one of the world's premiere chopper-building operations. Given his success in such a wide variety of endeavors, it's easy to imagine that Trotta would have succeeded in the music industry, too. Fortunately for chopper fans, he made a few detours from his original path.

Untitled

Untitled

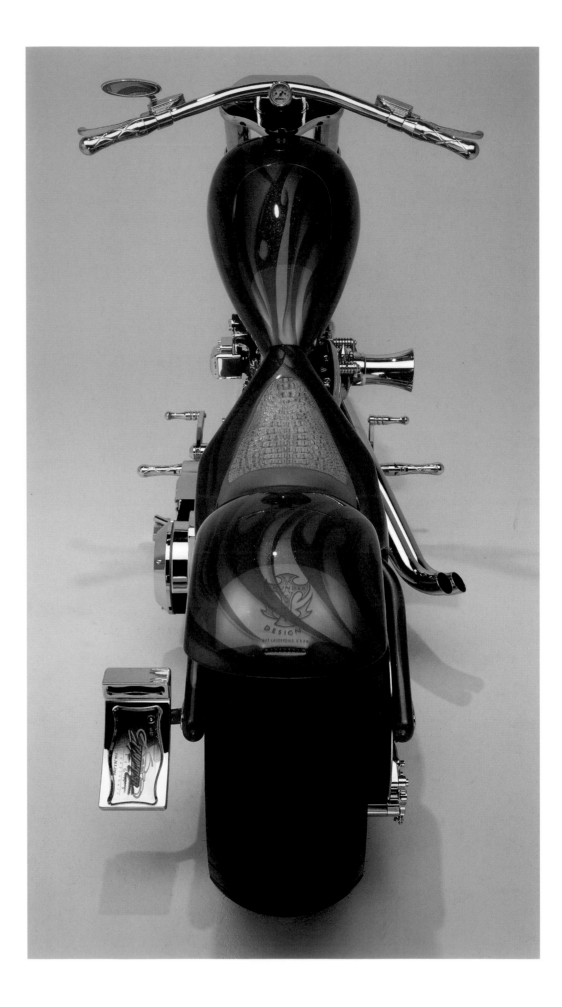

Untitled

Art Center College of Design
Library
1700 Lida Street
Pasadena, Calif. 91103

Untitled

Camel Bike '02

Chapter 20

Paul Yaffe

Unbridled Enthusiasm

A VARIETY OF MOTORCYCLE STYLES ARE REFERRED TO AS CHOPPERS. Paul Yaffe, one of the most celebrated chopper artists in the history of the genre, feels the important thing is how they make you feel and how they resonate with the past. Yaffe says, "A chopper is a vehicle that carries a certain kind of soul. It keeps a certain type of flame ignited. You have to hang with tradition. It's a sport. The whole idea is that you're supposed to build something and ride it."

Yaffe's work exhibits a sort of "nakedness," which is his word to illustrate the concept of less is more. His motorcycles are unencumbered with components that serve no purpose but decoration. He will try to find a way, if he can, to make one component do the job of three or four.

"Building a ground-up motorcycle is easier now, obviously, than ever," Yaffe says. But he makes a distinction between ground-up motorcycles and custom bikes. He markets his own signature Paul Yaffe Originals kit choppers through a catalog distributor. The only things missing are perspiration and paint. "Is it a custom bike?" he asks rhetorically. He says he doesn't really know how to answer that question, but he, personally, would never build the same bike twice. "Never!" he says. As an artist he can only find personal satisfaction by breaking the mold and creating something entirely new each time he begins a project. He also understands his responsibility to address the business side of the equation. "It's very difficult to make a living building one motorcycle at a time," Yaffe says.

"Ten years ago none of this existed," says Yaffe. "Everybody took stock bikes, and if you wanted a different rake or geometry, you'd cut the frame up and make yourself something. Every once in a while, someone would make a frame from scratch. But there were no big

fat tires, there were no billet parts, and there were no twelve different motors to choose from. It was all Harley stuff." He's always been a proponent of using genuine Harley-Davidson motors. He is one of the few master builders who prefers to use them; although, as he says, "I take them apart and give them horsepower." Yaffe likes horsepower, but not at the expense of reliability. He's also more of a fab-and-frame guy than a motor man; as he says, "Motors are easy."

"Riding for me is therapy," says Paul. He rides with the Hamsters, that group of not-so-scary bikers who all own custom sleds. The group was founded by his idols, Donnie Smith, Dave Perewitz, and Arlen Ness for whom his company, Paul Yaffe Originals, occasionally does sheet-metal work. "All these guys are my heroes. It's so cool to have them look to me sometimes for direction. That's a dream come true," Paul says.

At the age of 15, Paul began to teach himself the intricacies of motorcycle mechanics. His father used to let him tinker with an old Triumph chopper left over from the day. There was a gap of a few years when Paul lost interest in motorcycles and pursued less positive activities. As a young man he had serious bouts with drug and alcohol abuse. "I've done all the wrong shit for sure," he explains. "I never *went* to high school. I hung out at the back gate and sold drugs to the entire student body."

When he became clean and sober, Paul caught up again with motorcycles. For the next five years he continued to wrench in his spare time. His curriculum consisted of trial and error. For instance, he wanted to customize a bike by adding bullet turn signals. Paul telephoned the local Harley dealer and asked how much it would cost to install the them. They quoted $200, so he knew he could save that much by trying it himself. If he screwed up, the dealer could bail him out of trouble. He asked how much it would cost to hide wires inside his handlebars. The dealer quoted a price, and Paul tried to figure out how to do it himself first. He screwed up a lot, but he learned from his mistakes.

Yaffe's clients have a great deal of influence over the designs of the motorcycles he builds for them. He feels honored to be chosen to execute a great design, even if it's not entirely his own inspiration. For instance, the son of a colleague sent him a rendering that impressed him so much he decided to build it. Paul will turn the concept drawing into something that is rideable and do all the engineering. Ultimately, it will incorporate the PYO look and feel.

"It's a collaboration," Paul says, "but I'm very opinionated." He won't do anything that he doesn't think is cool. And he won't build a bike for someone he doesn't think is cool. "Money guys and celebrities think they can buy themselves the front of the line. The guys with the biggest money want the biggest discounts! It's funny the way that works. You cross a line and run smack into a wall with me. It just changes the whole dynamic of what we're doing." Those who become owners of PYO bikes also become Paul's friends. "You can't help but become buddies through this whole thing," he says.

As for the future of choppers, PYO is working on a new style of motorcycle. "Double Trouble" is a contemporary, high-end bike that features a lot of billet and radical components. Although he has stretched this bike farther than he has ever done before, he's going down four inches in the neck instead of going up five or six inches. The tank takes a downwards turn. It looks like a drag-racing bike: long, low, and stable enough to support wider tires and triple-digit horsepower.

When discussing radical choppers that combine huge motors and outrageous frame geometry, Yaffe laughs, "You're going to kill yourself! What is the point of that? If you ever actually used that kind of power the wind would get underneath and lift it right up. I make things that work and handle power. The [150-horsepower] motors are so out of balance and the bikes are so violent that they eat sheet metal, and they eat trannys, and they eat belts, and they eat brakes." Since he builds bikes that are meant to be ridden, the idea of building a bike just for show is ludicrous.

Yaffe thinks that a traditionalist approach from builders like Chica and Billy Lane keep the old-school flame burning and will continue to gain in popularity. "But you won't see any washing machine parts on my bikes," jokes Paul.

Bob Job

Untitled

Untitled

Chopper King

Untitled

Acknowledgments

I HADN'T WIELDED A CAMERA WITH SERIOUS INTENT FOR TEN YEARS WHEN I BEGAN THIS PROJECT. "It's like riding a bicycle," said all my friends. They had confidence I could do it again. But I had never photographed motorcycles before either. (That showed a lot of faith on my publisher's behalf.) So I studied as many existing studio photos of motorcycles I could find; and then I did a practice shoot with the help of Harold Pontarelli. It's a good thing too; because, before I could reshoot his bikes having learned a thing or two, he suffered a catastrophic theft. The best of his best were assembled at his shop to be transported to a studio in San Francisco when the unthinkable occurred. At least, now, some of them are on film.

I had intended initially to shoot portraits and bike illustrations all at one go, on an ad hoc basis from one location to the next. But I learned, for example, thanks to Harold, that the white paper backdrops I had intended to take along would not always work. They would rip to shreds at the slightest turn of a rubber tire. They were also impossible to keep clean and reuse for additional shoots. Moreover, the widest backdrop available was too narrow for the longest choppers.

It became evident right away that the issue of shooting bike illustrations at each portrait stop, that is at each builder's facility, was not going to work; there wasn't always enough room to set up a make-shift studio on location. Moreover, I had to make sure that the bikes would be there when I was. It turned out to be easier to assemble them at several studios around the country. That, in itself a logistical nightmare, was solved by Pam Hinojosa and Jody Pribyl who handled the pre-production chores while I traveled from place to place.

In spite of everything, I brought the paper. It was a good thing too, because I had to shoot several bikes on location after all; those we couldn't transport to a studio for one reason or another. My assistant, Tony Irvin, and I had to improvise often. For instance, we had to clear out the tables in the Olde Tymers Saloon in Bisbee, Arizona to shoot one of Pat Kennedy's choppers. Charlie Gahn and the gang made that otherwise impossible shot a reality. I rented a studio in Daytona Beach only to find out upon our arrival that the built-in cove wouldn't do. So we actually built a cyclorama, a seamless cove. Just the same, our efforts were almost scuttled by a severe storm and such severe humidity that the boards used to construct the cove warped overnight. The floor we built of wooden panels and so painstakingly screwed together and painted during a marathon construction period looked like a theatrical rendition of an undulating seascape the next morning. It had to be redone! I have Billy Collins, owner of Pyramax Studios, Eric Harvey, Pete "The Painter" Campanile, and Craig McDuffie to thank for making a hopeless situation work out at the eleventh hour—actually the twentieth hour.

The details of these adventures and more could be the topic of a book unto itself. Just the fact I was able to photograph so many examples of chopper art in such a short period of time under adverse circumstances is an accomplishment I think I can be proud of. By the way, I call them illustrations instead of photographs because I chose to add no artifice of my own. They are simply representations of each builder-artist's work, not mine. I make no claims of being a photographer of motorcycles; I'm a "people shooter." But watch out for Volume Two, now that I know what I'm doing!

It goes without saying that few undertakings of any quality are accomplished without the cooperation of many selfless individuals willing to give up their own time and, in many cases, contribute physical effort. These are the kinds of people who are motivated by kindness and grace, not personal gain. In other words, I couldn't have done this without them. So their names will be said.

In addition to those mentioned above, I want to thank Hank Bannister for lending more than an ear. Randy Bond provided his enthusiasm and encouragement. Mark Bradshaw of the Hideaway Grill in Cave Creek, Arizona made one portrait possible. Gerry Bybee lent clarity to my vision. Curt Cowan offered his sage advice as both a book guy and a bike guy. I'm going to thank Donnie Dacus, just because he has been a great friend for thirty-two years; and I figured he needed to see his name in print again. Thanks go to Bill Delzell for the use of Blue Sky Studios in San Francisco, and for explaining to the neighbors why crazy bikers were riding earsplitting choppers through the interior hallways. Thanks go to Bill and Lara Eichenberger for their generous hospitality. Rick Fairless of Easyriders Dallas made a rare chopper available. Joe Gibbs' proved that there's more than one way to scan a cat, or a photograph. Eileen Healy shed a special light on this project. Darwin Holmstrom saw fit to publish this book and remain a friend throughout the entire ordeal of making it real—and afterward. Samantha Isom and Prima Parsons applied themselves with astonishing vigor to assist when Tony Irvin, my full-time sidekick on the road had to return home temporarily to tend to family matters. For his valor at enduring the absence of his wife and daughter for so long—and for their permission to let me keep him for so long—I salute him. I owe my sanity to Reed and Penny Kailing for letting me decompress at the Rock 'n Roll Rest Home. Samy Kamienowicz provided more than just a flash of inspiration. Tom Kunhardt and John Mahaffey gave me both a canvas and a palette to paint with. Hail to Troy and Sarah Moore with their hearts as big as Texas and hospitality to match. Ed Phillips and Bob Kulesh helped me get a grip on things. Rich Patterson provided a sounding board for renditions of my text. Alan Schein was always available to listen to me complain. Paul Veale deserves kudos for his patience and for letting me use his trailer.

Sponsors

This book was made possible, in part, with the generous support of the following companies:

Eastman Kodak Company

Matthews Studio Equipment

Chimera Photographic Lighting

Blue Sky Rental Studios

Samy's Camera

Pyramax Studios

ART CENTER COLLEGE OF DESIGN LIBRARY

Index